How to use Jmol
to study
and present
molecular structures

Volume 1:
Learning to use Jmol
(basic and intermediate levels)

Angel Herráez

First edition: November 2007
© 2007, Angel Herráez.
All rights reserved.

ISBN 978-1-84799-259-8

To Michael Howard and Bob Hanson, as well as the rest of Jmol developers team, for giving Jmol away to the world.

To Eva and María Jesús, who provided the impetus for this book to finally come out.

To my fellow coworkers, Ana, Pilar, José Carlos, Cristina, Montse and Pepe, for their constant support in this crazy career of mine.

I express my heartfelt appreciation to Frieda Reichsman for revising the English translation.

About the author

The author has a BSc in chemistry and a PhD in biochemistry, and he is a lecturer of biochemistry and molecular biology at the University of Alcalá (Alcalá de Henares, Madrid, Spain). He has 9 years experience in building materials for teaching and study using computer-based molecular models (located at http://biomodel.uah.es/). He belongs to the BioROM working group – an interuniversity team devoted to creation and compilation of materials to assist in the learning of biochemistry, biotechnology and molecular biology – since its conception in 2000 (http://www.biorom.uma.es/). He is responsible for Spanish translations of the Jmol website and interface, and has contributed significantly to the contents of the website (both in English and Spanish) and of Jmol Wiki.

Table of contents

Foreword

The purpose of this book is to compile and organize information, both available from public sources and accumulated through experience, about the use of Jmol software, an interactive viewer for three-dimensional molecular models. The main objective is to provide a guide for those who are starting to take advantage of this program, without forgoing it as a handbook for more experienced users to consult and to progress. It is my hope that it might be useful to instructors, authors of teaching materials or popularization of science, students, researchers, and administrators or designers of information portals.

The guiding criterion followed while designing this handbook is to avoid a systematic and detailed description, in an encyclopedic format, of each and every possible action and command available in Jmol; such an approach corresponds to the official "reference guides" of the program, accessible in the internet. Due to the rapid evolution that Jmol is experiencing and to the fact that it is being developed by volunteers, the user-friendly documentation does not progress at the same pace, and that which is produced is rather technical, concise and fit for those who are already familiar with the software and with programming languages in general. More so, it is unlikely that a novice user will access information about capabilities whose existence he or she doesn't know of yet, or for which he or she does not know the relevant command. According to this – obviously personal – perception of the situation, as well as to the great diversity of actions possible in Jmol, the book has been organized in sections oriented with the aspiration of being useful for gradual, stepped learning and progress. Therefore, we start with the most easy-to-use commands and those which presumably will be needed more often, and then progressively advance into more rarely used commands, or those applicable only in specific fields, or those that are more difficult to comprehend and use. At the same time, occasionally in these pages I have given up the explanation of all possible ways of doing something, instead simplifying the description to a single one, advisable in my opinion for the sake of simplicity.

In order to attend to diverse readers' interests, the book contains sections devoted to those who need just an occasional and basic use of the software, another more advanced section explaining how to benefit from the scripting language – split up in two levels according to the already described approach, and continued in volume 2 – and, finally, a section not necessarily more complex but that will only be needed by those interested in preparing web pages to present models to third parties – this latter subdivided in three levels.

To benefit from this handbook, my advice is that each reader considers his/her aims and aspirations, and how much time (s)he is able to devote to learning and, therefore, tackle just those sections required, and do it gradually. There is much to explore and test in Jmol. It remains, obviously, to each reader's discretion to refrain or not from the impulse of studying all extensions of a command, developed over successive sections and linked by cross-references.

The contents in this handbook are tailored to version 11.2.x of Jmol. Some commands and variants here presented will not be valid for previous versions of Jmol, or may not act as described. In later versions of Jmol, all will foreseeably work as described here, but there is always the chance that some particular command will change its default behavior.

Finally, I remind the reader to look at the appendices, particularly the command index, the glossary and a list of reference internet addresses including that of the companion website created for this book – useful when (s)he needs to expand on this information, to pose questions to other users, or to learn from others and share experiences with them.

Conventions and notation used

Special fonts are used for those words that must be kept as they are written, as well as those corresponding to existing names and those that indicate something that must be written in their place.

- Options existing in the system (for example, menus or buttons in programs or in the operating system)

- **Filenames and paths**

- Source code (both HTML, JavaScript and Jmol scripting language); they are usually highlighted in bold type when they are keywords defined for the first time

- *A description that must be substituted by the desired value* (for example, where it says *filename*, one could write **model1.mol**; if it says *number*, one could write **5**)

- *Reference to that piece of information*

- **Variable information written by the user or author** (used in examples)

Regarding the use of keywords, numerical values, etc. in commands, please see also "Common features for commands and their parameters" (page 45).

Introduction

About 15 years ago, the possibility of showing and manipulating models of the structure of molecules became a reality for personal computers[1]. The development of computing equipment since that time has allowed great advances, increasing the capabilities of this software and simplifying its use, while the processing power and graphics management requirements mean no limitation for the computers nowadays commonplace in any office, home, briefcase or backpack.

One can question why it makes sense to handle a molecular model with a computer. For anyone who has approached this field, the answer likely needs little justification; it can be summarized in two words: availability and versatility. Although "physical" models are available, made of wood or plastic (typically either "ball and stick" or connected spheres), the chance of finding them in laboratories and classrooms is scarce; moreover, they are costly (probably due to low demand, and hence begetting a vicious circle) and, more importantly, they are limited: it is difficult to have enough pieces available to complete all molecules one needs to build. These three problems are solved if the model is built within the computer. In addition, the computerized model provides some valuable features with regard to the study or analysis of the structure. First, it perfectly suits large molecules, such as proteins and nucleic acids, not only because the computer cannot run out of parts, but also since it offers simplified renderings for these molecules. In the second place, it can be used not only individually, but also in front of a wide audience, thanks to computer-connected projecting equipment. Furthermore, the same material can be offered, for example, to students to revise and examine at leisure at

---

[1] In 1992, David and Jane Richardson presented the MAGE and PREKIN software programs, running on Macintosh computers. (D. C. Richardson & J. S. Richardson. The kinemage: A tool for scientific communication. *Protein Science* 1992 **1**: 3-9).

home during their study time, or even to the world in general through networks and the internet. Finally, it is tremendously interesting, from the standpoint of advancing knowledge and of learning, to have the ability to interact with the model, modifying not only the viewpoint or the size, but the type of rendering of the molecule, from the detail of the bond angles or the size of atoms to the abstraction of a polymeric chain's trajectory, its folding in space, or the shape and volume of a molecule as a whole.

Against this ideal scene just drawn, we must not neglect the consideration that models in the computer can also suffer from defects or limitations. For example, many people are impaired to some degree in three-dimensional perception from a flat illustration, despite lighting effects and simulation of interactive rotation. In any case, one's perception will always be less vivid than when accompanied by a tactile feeling. And, finally, in the case of teaching practice, we always confront the risk of so-called "video game effect": the visit of all screens in rapid succession without a true deepening of the understanding of structural information.

The fields where manipulation of three-dimensional computerized molecular models are used extend from, on one side, the study and teaching of chemistry, biochemistry, molecular biology, crystallography, materials science or nanotechnology through, on the other side, diverse research fields such as experimental results in crystallography, computational optimization of structures, the study of vibrational modes of molecules or their conformational changes, research on the structure of biomolecules and the interactions among them, the analysis of active centers, binding sites, contacts... and the list goes on.

What is the role of Jmol software in this context? Like other existing software, Jmol allows one to read molecular structure data, obtained externally by either experimental or theoretical means, and to display a virtual, three-dimensional model we can interact with. Given this, which features of Jmol make it suitable for our purposes against the set of other available programs? Two of the most prominent ones could be its cost – it is free – and the ability to use it under any operating system[2]. Other positive characteristics are its open-source nature, which endorses its availability, compatibility and evolution in the future[3], the great diversity of file formats it can read[4] (more than any other viewer of molecular structures) and its compatibility with materials prepared for other widespread programs[5] (namely, RasMol and Chime). Furthermore, it offers specific capabilities for several scientific areas and, technically, it is implemented under three variants, that respectively allow one to use it as a standalone application, to embed it within a web page and to integrate it as part of other programs.

It is not our aim to defend Jmol as a universal marvel or to despise other programs; in professional environments, those of researchers dedicated to the study of molecular structure, Jmol is surpassed by other programs in features and graphic quality. However, the accessibility of such programs to the general public – instructors included – is limited by the commercial nature of most of them, with an elevated price tag (justified by their performance), as well as, in some cases, by a greater difficulty of use (a greater ease if use is what is usually referred to as program "friendliness"). Finally, few of the programs can be integrated in web pages; this feature may seem barely significant, but it is that what allows instructors, and content authors in general, to build materials that can be used by people who don't have the program at their disposal and who have little or no experience in its use.

To further support the case for Jmol, we can also mention that it is one of the most commonly used viewers in the portals for querying structural databases[6] – particularly in those for biomolecules – and every day an increasing number of services and

---

[2] Jmol compatibility with different operating systems is explained on p. 17.

[3] The open source concept is explained and the legal conditions for using Jmol are specified on p. 17.

[4] You can look up a list of file formats accepted on p. 23.

[5] Such compatibility is detailed on p. 43.

[6] There is a commentary on databases and where to find them on p. 24.

web pages adopt it to display varied structures, with both teaching, disseminating and research purposes. During the last 3 years Jmol has undergone very rapid development, with frequent updates and additions of new features, and it profits from a very active community of programmers and users, who advocate sharing Jmol experience online, and hence facilitate learning the program.

Obtaining and deploying Jmol

Strictly speaking, Jmol doesn't need an installation or configuration. However, this section will serve as a guide for setting up this program and also for how to include Jmol within web pages we may create.

Downloading Jmol application and JmolApplet

Jmol is a free and open-source program. This means anyone can get it, use it, gain access to its source code, modify it or develop other programs that use it, as long as the new products so generated maintain identical licensing conditions. As far as this handbook is concerned, and without entering into technical and legal details (which are detailed on the GNU-LGPL license document), it suffices to say that Jmol can be downloaded, used, copied and distributed for free. Any web pages that we develop will include Jmol files, and the only legal requisite is that we also include with them the files that explain these conditions.

Jmol is written using the Java language, so it requires that the computer has Java installed[1]. This provides Jmol with the big advantage that it works on any operating system that supports Java (Windows, MacOS and Linux, among others).

The easiest way to install or update Java is to visit http://www.java.com/ and follow instructions. Mac users who use the "Automatic Update" feature have Java installed and updated automatically.

To obtain more information and to download Jmol, please visit its website, http://www.jmol.org/. There is also more specific information on the users community Wiki, http://wiki.jmol.org/.

It is important to distinguish between the different modes of Jmol. On one side, there is the standalone program, the **Jmol** "application", that is executed within its own window, as any other program installed on the computer. On the other side, we have an "applet", the **JmolApplet**, that can only be used when inserted or embedded in a web page. Otherwise, their features and functionality are almost identical. In the third place, although we won't deal with it in this book, there is also a variant of Jmol in the form of a component (also termed a Java library) that can be included within other programs, called the **JmolViewer**.

The complete program is obtained as a compressed package (you have a choice between **tar.gz** and **zip** formats), most usually from the website, www.jmol.org. You must decompress it on your hard disk, so these files will turn up as a result:

Jmol.jar	The standalone program, or **Jmol** application.
Jmol.js	A collection of functions written in JavaScript (a Javascript library), that facilitates writing web pages that use the applet.
JmolApplet.jar	The applet **JmolApplet**, on a single piece (monolithic).
JmolApplet0.jar and other files which names start with **JmolApplet0** and end with **.jar**	The applet **JmolApplet**, split up so that its loading is faster.
JmolAppletSigned.jar **JmolAppletSigned0.jar** and other files which names start with **JmolAppletSigned0** and end with **.jar**	The "signed" versions of the former. This is an issue of security rules in Java: the signed applet may access files in other parts of our hard disk and other web servers, once we have authorized it.

COPYRIGHT.txt **LICENSE.txt** **README.txt**	Files with information about Jmol package, terms of use, copy and distribution.
jmol **jmol.bat** **jmol.mac** **jmol.sh**	Files to start up the program under different operating systems.

For the purposes covered in this handbook, you only need to worry about those files whose name has been boxed. To legally fulfill the conditions in the GNU-LGPL license, you must also include the three informative files in any distribution you make.

Note 1: Java terminology is rather confusing; Java installation goes by three different names:

- JVM, or Java Virtual Machine
- JRE, or Java Runtime Environment
- Java plug-in

You don't usually need to install JDK (Java Development Kit); this is only necessary if you want to develop your own Java programs.

Preparation for using Jmol

According to what has been described above, there are two possible environments for using Jmol:

- **Jmol** application: as a standalone program, mainly for personal use, studying diverse aspects of the structure of molecules. It is also useful for testing during development of web pages.

- **JmolApplet**: to prepare web pages that will mainly be used by others. A remarkable scenario is the development of materials for teaching or popularization of science.

Preparation for using the standalone Jmol application

For this purpose, you just need the **Jmol.jar** file, contained within the downloaded Jmol package. To open or execute it, it is usually enough to double-click on it, since the operating system will already have associated **jar** files with the installed version of Java runtime environment. Anyhow, since there is not a standard installation procedure for Jmol as for other typical programs (for example, it will not show up on the Start > Programs menu), a description follows with some tricks that allow a more convenient use.

Creation of a shortcut for Jmol

(This description is for the Windows operating system)

Locate the folder where you decompressed the Jmol package; in it, find the **Jmol.jar** file and create a shortcut for it (e.g., using the mouse right button menu); you can later place that shortcut where you prefer (Windows desktop, programs menu, etc.).

Association of model files with Jmol

(This description is for the Windows operating system)

In the same way indicated here for **pdb** files, this can also be done for other extensions (**mol, xyz, cml**...) accepted by Jmol.

On Windows Explorer (or file manager), choose from the menu Tools > Folder options > File types > pdb > Advanced options > Actions > New >

- Under Action, type, for example:
  open with Jmol

- Under Application used, type:
  "C:\Program files\Java\bin\javaw.exe" -jar
  "C:\Program files\Jmol\Jmol.jar" "%1"

Type all in the same line, including quotes and replacing **C:\Program files\Java** with the specific path to where Java is installed on your computer, and **C:\Program files\Jmol** with the path to your decompressed Jmol package (or else where you have decided to locate **Jmol.jar**).

Preparation for using the JmolApplet

Copy the **Jmol.js** file and all **.jar** files whose names start with **JmolApplet0** to the root folder of what will be your website.

Continue with directions given under "Including Jmol models in a web page" (p. 97).

While designing your web pages, you will want to work with models to choose the ways you want to display them, to test the results of commands, etc. For that purpose, it may be more convenient to use the application to make these decisions, before putting the models into the web pages via the Jmol applet.

Obtaining molecular models

Virtual "molecular models" in the computer are three-dimensional representations built by Jmol (or other similar programs) from molecular coordinate files that contain the identities of all atoms in the molecule and their coordinates in space.

Different formats can be used to specify such information in a molecular coordinate file. Thanks to its open-source character, Jmol has been progressively expanded to understand all those formats (if anyone knows about a new format, (s)he can contribute by adding it or requesting that Jmol developer team does so). The ability of Jmol to interpret the file relies upon its contents, not its file extension.

Coordinate files are usually plain text files, although it is common to compress them using the **gzip** format, which is automatically recognized and decompressed on the fly by Jmol.

The most frequently used formats are **pdb** for macromolecules (proteins and nucleic acids) and **mol** or **xyz** for small molecules. This is a more or less complete listing of formats supported by Jmol:

- **ADF**: Amsterdam Density Functional files
- **Agl**: XML files from ArgusLab
- **C3XML**: XML files from Chem3D
- **CIF / mmCIF**: crystallographic information file and macromolecular crystallographic information file, standard formats from the International Union of Crystallography
- **CML**: chemical markup language
- **CSF**: chemical structure from Fujitsu CACHe and Fujitsu Sygress
- **CTFile**: chemical table from Elsevier MDL

- **GAMESS**: output format from General Atomic and Molecular Electronic Structure System, Gordon Research Group, Iowa State University
- **Gaussian** 94/98/03, output format from Gaussian, Inc.
- **HIN**: HyperChem from Hypercube, Inc.
- **Jaguar** from Schrodinger, LLC
- **MM1GP**: molecular mechanics from Ghemical
- **MOL**: structure, from Elsevier MDL
- **MOL2**: structure, from Sybyl
- **MOLPRO**: output XML format from Molpro
- **MOPAC**: output formats mopout and graphf from MOPAC 93/97/2002/2007 (public domain)
- **NWCHEM**: output format from NWChem, Pacific Northwest National Laboratory
- **Odydata**: data from Odyssey, WaveFunction, Inc.
- **PDB**: standard format from Protein Data Bank, Research Collaboratory for Structural Bioinformatics
- **QOUT**: from Q-Chem, Inc.
- **SDF**: structure (with several models) from Elsevier MDL
- **SHELX**: from Structural Chemistry Department, University of Göttingen (Germany)
- **SMOL**: data from Spartan, Wavefunction, Inc.
- **Xodydata**: XML data from Odyssey, WaveFunction, Inc.
- **XYZ**: XMol file from Minnesota Supercomputer Institute
- **XYZ+vib**: XYZ format with vibration vector information
- **XYZ-FAH**: XYZ file from the Folding@home project

Models from databases

The most common way to obtain coordinate files is by going to molecular structure databases; the suitability of each one of them depends on the field of work (biochemistry, organic or inorganic chemistry, crystallography, etc.). You can look up a list of databases and links to them in this handbook's companion website.

Models from web pages

A second option is to copy a model already displayed on a web page (you can often do so from a web page that uses either a Jmol applet or the MDL Chime plug-in). In this case, it is important to check and honor the copyright in the original page.

If the model is displayed using Chime, you just need to right-click (i.e., click using the  mouse right button) – or hold down the button on a single-button mouse –, and Chime menu will pop-up; then choose **File** > **Save molecule as...** and you can choose path and filename to save the file (retaining the original format).

If the model is displayed using Jmol, open the pop-up menu (by clicking while you hold the **Ctrl** key, or by clicking with the right button, or else clicking on the bottom-right "**Jmol**" logo). Then, choose the topmost entry (that shows the model title) and then the last one from those that show up (**View** followed by the filename). Then, depending on how your browser is configured, one of these things will happen: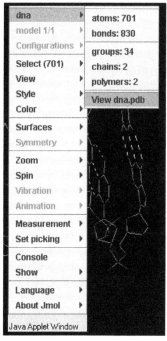

- an "open or save" type dialog will be shown;

- the model will be opened using the default program:

  - if RasMol: you need to open the menu, **File** > **Save**;

  - if Chime: the method has been explained above;

- the coordinate file will be opened as text in the browser; in this case, just use the browser's menu, **File** > **Save as** >

Text file and make sure it has the proper extension (**mol**, **pdb**, **xyz**...) so that it is easier to identify later.

Building models

It is possible to create molecular models for simple molecules using several chemical formula drawing or conformational optimization programs. As an example of a program free of charge (only for Windows environment) that allows one to easily draw formulas and convert them into a three-dimensional plausible model, we can mention and recommend *ChemSketch Freeware*, from ACD/Labs (Advanced Chemistry Development Inc.; http://www.acdlabs.com/). In addition to a simple and intuitive use, it offers the advantage of including an ample collection of predesigned formulas, from which with little modification it is easy to get the desired molecule. The program also provides an algorithm for three-dimensional optimization, after which the model can be saved in **mol** format, readable by Jmol.

Basic operation of the program from the interface

Interface language

One of the favorable characteristics of Jmol – and a consequence of its open-source nature – is the availability of the user interface in several languages. Java takes care of choosing the language automatically to match that of the operating system, although it is possible to impose another:

- From the pop-up menu (which use is explained on p. 34), one up from the last entry is **Language** and offers a choice of those available (at the moment, Catalan, Czech, Dutch, English, Estonian, French, German, Portuguese, Brazilian Portuguese, Spanish and Turkish). Choosing a language has an immediate effect (it may be delayed a little since the program must reload), but it is not advisable to change language repeatedly as this can lock up the system.

- From the script console, from a script file or from a web page, this command is available:

  language = *code*

  using the standard 2-character language *code* (es, en, fr, pt, de...)

- While starting the application from a command line, you can use the -Duser.language= parameter followed by the 2-character language code; for example:

  ```
  java -Duser.language=en -jar Jmol.jar
  ```
  for English.

- The same result as in the former option, but for the applet, is achieved in a permanent way by modifying Java options:

    1. Open Windows control panel (a similar procedure is likely available in other operating systems);

    2. Look for the **Java** icon (it may be inside the **Other Control Panel options** group) and double-click on it;

    3. Under the **Java** tab, choose **Runtime Java Applet config**. In the **JRE** row corresponding to the latest version, click on the textbox located under **Parameters** and type

       ```
       java -Duser.language=en
       ```

       (or another language code instead of en)

Top menu

This menu, located at the top of the application window, offers a limited number of  features. Most of them are duplicated on the pop-up menu, so they will not be described here; we will concentrate on those actions exclusive to the application, not available from the pop-up menu.

Loading files

File > Open and **File > Open URL** allow you to load a molecular model or a script file, either from a local disk or from an internet address.

Saving files

File > Export > Export Image or Script allows you to save to disk a snapshot of the current view of the model (a 24-bit color image, in **jpg**, **png** or **ppm** format), or else to export the current state of the model as a script file (with **spt** extension by default). The script file can be later loaded using File > Open, and it will restore the model to the same display and orientation.

File > Export > Render in POV-Ray allows you to save to disk a file readable by POV-Ray (ray tracing software with high quality, three-dimensional vector graphics).

File > Export > Export PDF allows you to save to disk a snapshot of the current view of the model in **pdf** format (Adobe's Portable Document Format).

Copying information

Edit > Copy Image copies a snapshot of the current view of the model to the clipboard (which can then be pasted to any program that accepts images).

Other functions

File > Script opens a window, the "script console", where you can type commands in Jmol scripting language, as well as get information from the model. Its use is described in later sections.

File > New opens a new empty program window.

File > Close or File > Exit close the Jmol window.

Mouse and keyboard

Basic operation

Manipulation of the mouse, with either one or several buttons, together with some keys (**Shift** or ⇧, **Ctrl**, **Alt**) is the most basic and simplest way of moving and orienting the molecular model. The following figure summarizes the available actions. Note that every action can be achieved with 3, 2 or just one button mouse.

	Main button (left)	Middle button	Secondary button (right)
Rotate around X,Y	🖱️✛ drag		
Rotate around Z	🖱️ ↔ hold Shift while dragging horizontally	🖱️ ↔ drag horizontally	🖱️ ↔ hold Shift while dragging horizontally (may fail on Mac's)
Zoom	🖱️ ↕ hold Shift while dragging vertically	🖱️ ↕ drag vertically	
	or use mouse wheel 🖱️		
Move along X,Y (= translate)	🖱️ ✛ hold Shift while double-clicking and holding down on the second click for dragging	🖱️ ✛ double-click, holding down on the second click for dragging	🖱️ ✛ hold Ctrl while dragging
	you can click either on the molecule or away from it		
Restore & center	🖱️ hold Shift while double-clicking	🖱️ double-click	
	you must click away from the molecule		
Open Jmol menu	🖱️ hold Ctrl while clicking or click on Jmol logo Jmol		🖱️ click

On the other hand, if the pointer is hovered over one of the atoms (holding it steady for a moment), a floating box, or tooltip, will show up with the atom's identification.

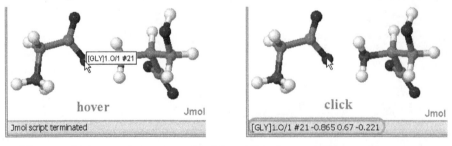

hover   Jmol   click   Jmol

Jmol script terminated   [GLY]1.O/1 #21 -0.865 0.67 -0.221

If you click on the atom, its identification and coordinates are shown in the script console[1] (application and applet); in the case of the applet, the same information usually appears also in the browser's status line (at the bottom of the window)[2].

Note 1: This is the default behavior, but it can be altered if either Measurement or Set picking in the menu, or the set picking command, have been used.

Note 2: Display of text in the status line may be blocked depending on configuration of the browser.

Advanced options

Many of the following possibilities depend on previous commands of Jmol scripting language, applied either at the console or from a script included in a web page. Details are explained in those sections devoted to scripting language, either here or in volume 2.

Atom identification

As already pointed out, hovering the cursor or clicking provides information about any atom. The precise information shown when hovering can be controlled, or even suppressed altogether, from the console or from a web page by using the **hover** command (described in volume 2).

Picking

The default action when clicking the mouse on an atom is to identify it, as it has been mentioned. Nonetheless, it is possible to exchange identification for many other actions, either through the menu, Set picking or Measurement, or using the **set picking** command (described in volume 2). For example, clicking an atom can:

- display distances, angles or torsions
- attach labels
- draw lines between atoms (monitor lines)
- select the atom or else the residue, chain or molecule to which it belongs
- select all atoms from the same chemical element

- define the atom as new rotation center for the model (and, optionally, center it within the panel)
- modify drawn objects
- make the molecule spin around an internal axis

Among all these options, one is directly accessible without any menu or scripts: measurement of distances, angles and torsions, composed of drawing monitor lines plus labeling them with a measurement (these concepts are explained on p. 92). To such purpose, you must double-click on an atom to start the measurement and double-click on another to finish it. Between those two events, a temporary line and measurement are displayed (called "rubberbands"[1], since they follow the pointer); the steps in the measurement process are:

1. Double-click on the starting atom.
2. As the pointer is moved, a rubberband extends from that atom to the pointer, until the pointer hovers over another atom, when a provisional measurement is displayed.
3. If you double-click on the second atom, both the monitor line and the measurement are set, and the measurement process ends.
4. If you single-click on the second atom, the provisional measurement continues for angles, with a second rubberband.
5. If you then double-click on a third atom, the monitor line and the angle measurement are set, and the process ends.
6. If you single-click on the third atom, the provisional measurement continues for torsions (dihedral angles), with a new rubberband.
7. The provisional measurement of torsions continues until you double-click on a fourth atom, setting the monitor line and the torsion measurement.

Note 1: By default, rubberbands are colored fuchsia, but this can be changed using the `color rubberBand` command. Once the measurement is set, the line becomes white or black, whichever contrasts with the background color (or else the color specified using `color measures`).

Section through the model

It is possible to section or cut through the model (called slabbing) in order to hide what is in front – or, at your choice, behind – the cutting plane and hence appreciate details inside the molecule. This special mode requires a previous activation from the console or a script in the web page, using the **slab on** command (volume 2). Once slabbing is activated, there are two cutting planes, front and rear, which can be shifted using **slab** and **depth** commands or using the mouse, as described in next figure.

	Main button (left)	Middle button	Secondary button (right)
	These only work if previously activated with a slab on command:		
Slab from the front	Ctrl ✪ ↕ hold Ctrl and Shift while dragging vertically ✱		
Slab from the rear	Ctrl ✪ ↕ hold Ctrl and Shift while double-clicking & dragging on the second click vertically ✱		
Shift the slab (keeping constant thickness)	Alt Ctrl ✪ ↕ hold Alt, Ctrl and Shift while dragging vertically ✱		
	✱ if they fail on a Mac, try clicking first, then holding the key, then drag		

Spinning around internal axes

The mouse can launch continuous spinning of the model around an internal axis, defined by a line previously drawn with a draw command (which is described in Volume 2).

- If you click on one of the line ends, the molecule starts spinning (counterclockwise as seen from that end).
- If you click on the other end, it spins in the opposite direction (also counterclockwise if seen from the clicked end).
- Spinning is stopped by clicking again on any line end.
- The direction of spinning is clockwise if the **Shift** key is held while clicking.

Navigation through the model

Navigation mode involves a special operation of movement and perspective where it is possible to travel inside the model, loosing sight of whatever is left behind; it is something akin to virtual reality systems. Once activated, the keyboard is used to "navigate". Due to its specialized nature, it is not described in this handbook; there is a detailed technical description in the official interactive scripting documentation and in http://chemapps.stolaf.edu/jmol/docs/misc/navigation.pdf

Pop-up menu

This menu is shared by the application and applet, and offers a wide assortment of options (without reaching, however, the full power provided by the scripting language through the console).

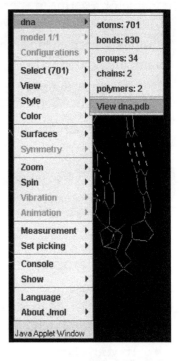

There are 3 ways to open this menu:

- "**right-click**": place the mouse pointer on any part of the Jmol panel and press the secondary button of the mouse (this is usually the right-hand button);

- "**click on logo**": place the mouse pointer on the **Jmol** logo located at the bottom-right corner of the Jmol panel, and press the main button of the mouse (usually, the left-hand button);

- "**Ctrl+click**": place the mouse pointer on any part of Jmol panel, hold the **Ctrl** key and press the main button of the mouse (usually, the left-hand button).

(methods 2 and 3 allow for use of Jmol with single-button mice, common on Macintosh computers)

We won't expand here on describing this menu, since it is rather intuitive and self-explanatory; only those operations presumably used most frequently will be commented on briefly.

Note: If you want to explore details and possibilities of each option in the pop-up menu, follow this method, which displays the commands for you to see, after Jmol executes them: open the script console (using the top menu > File > Script or using the pop-up menu > Console), then carry out one operation using the menu, then go back to the console (by clicking in it), and finally, press the up-arrow key on the keyboard; the console will display the last command executed by Jmol, which matches that option in the menu; for additional details about the commands used, check the relevant subsection in the sections devoted to description of Jmol scripting language.

Information about the molecule

Once a file with a molecular model has been loaded, Jmol's pop-up menu offers information about its composition:

- The topmost entry in the pop-up menu shows the molecule name and the number of atoms, bonds, groups, chains and polymers it contains.

- The **Model** sub-menu displays information in the case of multimodel files, or when several files have been loaded.

- The **Configurations** sub-menu offers, if applicable, the alternate positions of some atoms[1].

- The **Select** sub-menu includes the number of atoms currently selected.

- The **Select > Element** sub-menu provides a list of the chemical elements that comprise the model.

- The **Select > Protein / Nucleic** sub-menus provide lists of residue names contained[1].

- The **Select > Hetero > By HETATM** gives a list of the prosthetic groups[1] in the file.

Note 1:   Only for **pdb** format files or equivalent, with molecules that include such information.

Atom style

Atoms are rendered as spheres, whose reference size is the van der Waals radius of each element[1].

- **Style > Scheme > CPK Spacefill** gives a full-size representation, as spheres or spacefilling model (100% van der Waals).

- **Style > Scheme > Ball and Stick** is the classic style, with balls at 20% van der Waals radius (and sticks 0.15 Å in diameter).

- **Style > Atoms > % van der Waals** allows you to choose other sizes.

Color of the spheres is set using **Color > Atoms**. In addition, they can be made – or not – translucent, i.e. semitransparent, with **Color > Atoms > Translucent / Opaque**.

For higher flexibility in choosing size and color, the `spacefill` and `color` commands are available in the scripting language (p. 51 and 54).

All structural items (bonds and others) inherit by default their color, visibility, selection state, etc. from associated atoms.

A variation for representing atoms is to use dotted surface spheres. In this case, the command is located on the **Surfaces > Dot Surface** menu.

Note 1: Atomic and ionic radii used by Jmol can be looked up at the companion website.

Bond style

Bonds are rendered as sticks (cylinders), and are associated with both atoms joined.

- **Style > Scheme > Wireframe / Sticks / Ball and Stick** use, respectively, thin lines, 0.3 Å cylinders and 0.15 Å cylinders in diameter.

- **Style > Bonds > n Å** offer other thicknesses.

The bond color is initially that of the two atoms it joins (each half of the bond takes one color), but another color can be imposed for the whole bond using **Color > Bonds**. Moreover, they can be made – or not – translucent, i.e. semitransparent, with **Color > Bonds > Translucent / Opaque**.

For additional options, `wireframe` and `color bonds` commands are available in the scripting language (p. 52 and 74).

Schematic renderings for biomolecules

Biological macromolecules (proteins, nucleic acids and, in limited form, carbohydrates) in **pdb**, **mmcif** or equivalent file formats can be rendered in simplified representations that restrict visualization to the trajectory of the polymer. They are favorable for appreciating the folding of the chain in space and its secondary structure. On them, the trajectory is defined as the series of main atoms in the backbone: alpha carbons on a protein and phosphorus atoms on a nucleic acid.

When called from the pop-up menu, the different schematic variants are mutually exclusive, as well as with the spacefill, wireframe, sticks, and ball and stick schemes.

The menu to use is **Style > Structures >**

- **Backbone** draws a zigzag line connecting the atoms that define trajectory.

- **Trace** draws a smooth curve passing through middle points between successive atoms in the trajectory.

- **Ribbons** draws a solid flat ribbon, following the same trajectory as the trace.

- **Strands** are similar to ribbons, but formed by longitudinal parallel threads.

- **Cartoon** draws ribbons in those stretches with alpha or beta secondary structure, and trace in the remainder; each stretch ends with an arrowhead (C or 3' terminus).

- **Rockets** draws cylinders for alpha stretches, planks for beta stretches and trace for the remainder; cylinders and planks are always straight and end with an arrowhead.

- **Cartoon Rockets** is a variant of **cartoon** where the alpha stretches are cylinders and the beta stretches are ribbons.

(For more details and options, check the commands with the same name, on the scripting language sections, p. 52 and vol. 2.)

The **Cartoon** and **Trace** options available from **Style > Scheme** apply in addition a secondary structure coloring scheme.

The color of each type of schematic rendering is controlled separately using **Color > Structure**.

Colors

The **Color** menu offers all "objects" available in Jmol and, for each of them, a list of predefined colors. For **Atoms** and **Structures**, it also provides **By scheme** coloring patterns (illustrated on the back cover and in one of the appendices):

- **Element (CPK)** is the initial and default option; assigns a particular color to each element, following the so-called "CPK scheme" (from Corey, Pauling and Koltun).

- **Molecule:** each group of atoms connected by bonds constitutes a "molecule" (as interpreted by Jmol, not indicated by the coordinate file) that receives a different color.

- **Formal / Partial charge:** reads the value of charge assigned to each atom in the file and uses a color gradient from red (negative charge) to white (no charge) to blue (positive charge).

- **Amino Acid:** each one receives its own color according to the "amino" scheme (see appendix and back cover) [1].

- **Secondary Structure:** in proteins, colors the alpha helix stretches fuchsia, the beta strands orange-yellow, the turns blue and the rest white; in nucleic acids, colors DNA purple and RNA reddish [1].

- **Chain:** all atoms with the same chain identifier receive the same color [1].

- **Inherit:** by default, all "objects" take the color of their associated atoms; this option allows you to restore that coloring.

(For more details, check the coloring subsections on the scripting language sections, p. 54 and 74.)

Note 1: Only on file formats that provide such information: **pdb**, **mmcif** or equivalent.

Selecting parts of the molecule

It is key to bear in mind that every action (styles, colors, etc.) affects just the portion of the molecule that is currently in a selected state. Initially, all atoms are selected, but that state can be later modified by using the **Select** menu:

- **Element** will select all atoms of the element chosen from a list with those comprising the molecule;

- **Protein** will select all protein atoms based on interpretation of the "atom identifier" notations in the molecular coordinate file [1];

- **Nucleic** is similarly based on interpretation of the "atom identifiers" [1];

- **Hetero** matches "heterogen groups", that is, those labeled as HETATM in the file (usually, all atoms that are not protein or nucleic acid) [1]; we will refer to them as prosthetic groups;

- **Carbohydrate:** only some residues are recognized, by their name [1];

- **None of the above**: whatever does not fit into any of the 4 categories above.

As an aid during selection, we can use:

- **Select > ☑Selection halos** highlights the currently selected atoms, encircling them in orange;

- **Select > ☑Display selected only** hides atoms not currently selected.

It is also possible to select atoms one by one using the mouse: **Set picking > Select**; that selection is cumulative and to remove an atom from the selected set it must be "picked" (i.e., clicked) again.

Note 1: Only for file formats that provide such information, such as **pdb**, **mmcif** or equivalent.

Hydrogen atoms

With a single click it is possible to hide or show again all hydrogen atoms: **Style > Atoms > ☑Show Hydrogens**. This action controls their visibility independently of other options or styles, and is particularly useful in simplifying the appearance of large molecules.

Labels on atoms

We can tag any atom with a label that remains associated with it, under **Style > Labels**. You can choose between labeling with the name and/or number that identifies that atom in the file, or the element symbol. Similarly to other actions, only the currently selected atoms will be labeled.

It is also possible to label atoms as they are being pointed at with the mouse: **Set picking > Label** (in this case, it is not possible to choose the type of label).

To choose their characteristics, we have **Color > Labels** and **Style > Labels > Position Label on Atom**.

Measurements

As already pointed out under the "Picking" heading within mouse operation (p. 31), distances and angles can be measured without any previous operation, just by double-clicking on an atom, then single-clicking on successive ones and double-clicking on the last one. Alternatively, this may be done using options in the menu:

Measurement > Click for distance / angle / torsion measurement To measure a distance, the program waits until we click on 2 successive atoms; for an angle, on 3; for a dihedral or torsion angle, on 4 atoms. The units used for distances can be chosen using **Measurements > Distance units...**

Default option is restored with **Measurement > Double-Click begins and ends all measurements** (its use is described under "Picking", p. 31).

Three-dimensional perception

In order to assist in perceiving the model in 3 dimensions, some options are available to adjust perspective and to use stereographic images:

- **Style > ☑Perspective Depth** uses conical perspective, so that what is farther away is reduced;

- **Style > ☐Perspective Depth** uses orthogonal perspective, without any depth effect;

- **Style > Stereographic >...** generates a stereographic image:

    - by means of 2 side-by-side images, prepared either for "cross-eyed", or convergent, vision or for "wall-eyed", or divergent, vision;

    - by using two slightly shifted images, adequate for two-color glasses (red and blue, red and cyan, red and green)

Coordinate system and crystallographic information

- **Style > ☑Axes** draws the Cartesian axes of the coordinate system of atoms in the file.

- **Style > ☑Bound Box** draws a parallelogram around the molecule.

- **Style > ☑Unit Cell** for models that include crystallographic information, draws the unit cell and displays its parameters as text (at the upper left corner).

The thickness and color of the lines can be controlled with:

- **Style > Axes / Boundbox / Unitcell > ...**
- **Color > Axes / Boundbox / Unitcell > ...**

(Commands related to crystalline systems are much more versatile, but due to their specialized nature they are left for volume 2.)

Jmol scripting language

Introduction to commands in Jmol

Loading a molecular model file, determining its orientation and movement, its rendering style, visibility of its parts, color…, in summary, all that can be done in Jmol, is controlled using commands that constitute the so-called Jmol "scripting language". The word **script** refers to a series of instructions to follow; the program (application or applet) "reads" those commands one at a time, interprets them and applies them to the model.

Jmol has inherited most of the commands that form the scripting language of the RasMol and Chime programs, but adds to them many others which are new and exclusive to Jmol.

All that is done in Jmol using either mouse and keyboard or the menus is internally converted into commands in this language. Furthermore, many actions are only possible through the commands; therefore, the scripting language is the most powerful tool for using Jmol – also, the most complex to master completely. Due to its amplitude, in this handbook we have chosen to split its description into sections or levels, starting from those commands easiest to use and which presumably will be more often needed, to later and gradually advance towards commands that will be less frequently used, or which are applied only in specific fields, or which are more difficult to understand and to use. Even so, some commands that have been considered the most advanced will still remain out of the coverage of this handbook, and the reader interested in working thoroughly with Jmol should go to the official guide, the "interactive scripting documentation", available at the Jmol website where, in a "reference guide" style, all available commands are explained as well as all the options they can take.

Commands can be issued manually, by typing them one at a time at the "script console", or else written into a text file ("script file") that is saved to disk and then loaded into or read by Jmol.

The script can also be written as part of the source code of a web page that includes the **JmolApplet**. In the two latter modes, the commands become a script, which is a way to program actions for the molecular model.

Issuing commands

As has just been mentioned, commands for Jmol can be supplied in diverse ways:

- **Directly, from the console**: typing them into the console, either in the application or the applet; they can be typed and executed one at a time, or else as a series of commands – separated with a semicolon – and later all executed in one go.

- **From script files**: commands are the content of a text file, which Jmol loads either from the top menu **File** > **Open** or by a `script` command. If several commands are chained (issued in sequence), they must be separated with a semicolon or a line break.

- **Using JavaScript variables**: within the source code of a web page, commands can be provided as the value assigned to a JavaScript variable; the browser provides connectivity between JavaScript and Java, effectively passing the commands to Jmol, either directly as the page is built or as a consequence of a later action, for example when the user presses a button included in the page.

- **From a simulated console in the web page**: finally, it is also possible to build within the web page a form control, of textbox type, where the user can type commands which will be transmitted to the Jmol applet embedded in that same page. (See `jmolCommandInput` function in **Jmol.js** library, described in the section for the web edition, level 3, p. 114.)

Common features for commands and their parameters

Plural forms

For many commands, Jmol accepts as synonyms the singular and plural forms. Examples: cartoon, halo, hBond, label, measure, measurement, meshRibbon, monitor, ribbon, rocket, selectionHalo, ssBond, star, strand, vector. Exceptions: dots, trace, backbone.

This happens similarly with British and American variants of spelling: centre = center, colour = color.

Uppercase and lowercase

In this handbook some capitalization is used as a means to improve readability of those commands composed of several joined words. However, Jmol does not distinguish between uppercase and lowercase, so it is irrelevant how the commands are typed. Examples: hBond = hbond = Hbond, meshRibbon = meshribbon.

Types of parameters and expressions

Commands in Jmol scripting language use different kinds of parameters or arguments; their common features are reviewed next.

Numerical values

When a numerical parameter sets dimensions for atoms, bonds or schematics, an integer is interpreted as "RasMol units", equivalent to 1/250 of an angstrom. In contrast, numbers that include a decimal point are interpreted as angstroms (1 Å = 10^{-10} m). So, for example, spacefill **2** will render tiny spheres (2/250 = 0.008 Å radius), while spacefill **2.0** will produce spheres of radius 2 Å.

For dimensions corresponding to drawn objects (axes, draw, vector...), integers are generally interpreted as pixels and decimals as angstroms.

Times (in commands for movement) are always read as seconds.

Angles of rotation are interpreted as sexagesimal degrees, and speeds of rotation or spinning, as degrees per second.

Logical or Boolean values: activation or inactivation

Several commands set variables whose state is toggled between active and inactive. In these cases, Jmol admits the keywords **on** and **true** for the active state, and **off** and **false** for the inactive state. (Occasionally, a numeric value may be read as false if zero, or true otherwise, but it is better not to trust such behavior in general.)

Colors

Colors can be set using a name (e.g. **yellow**), a code ([128,255,0] or [x88FF00]), or a coloring scheme (**amino**). Look up the subsections "Coloring commands", in level 1 and 2 sections, for more details. You can also check the colors used by Jmol in the appendix and on the back cover.

Atom expressions

In order to change the type of rendering of a molecular model, for example to focus attention on a certain part, etc., it is necessary to refer to the constituting atoms. Such references are generically called "atom expressions". On some commands (select, restrict, hide, display...) they can be issued directly, but on the more complex ones atom expressions must be enclosed in parentheses (). If in doubt, it is always safe to use the parentheses.

Both the level 1 section and volume 2 contain subsections describing the available atom expressions; in addition, the details of using some of them will be introduced gradually in the paragraphs devoted to relevant commands.

Coordinates

Jmol uses 3 types of coordinates:

- Absolute XYZ, external or associated with the Jmol panel. On some commands they can be issued as 3 consecutive numbers (separated by spaces), but on most of them they must be surrounded by braces **{ }** and separated by either spaces or commas. The units are angstroms.

  Examples: **{1 2 0} {0.83 -1.34 2.0} {-1.2, 2.1, 0}**

- Internal XYZ or associated to the model's coordinate system. As with the former, on some commands they can be issued as 3 consecutive numbers (separated by spaces), but on most of them they must be surrounded by braces **{ }** and separated by either spaces or commas. The units are angstroms.

  Examples: **{1 2 0} {0.83 -1.34 2.0} {-1.2, 2.1, 0}**

- Fractional, relative to the unit cell in models with crystallographic information (therefore, internal but using different axes and scale). They are identified as such by including at least one fraction, that is, a **/** sign. They must be surrounded by braces **{ }** and separated by either spaces or commas. The units are those of the unit cell.

  Examples: **{1,1/2,-1} {-2 1 -1/1} {1/1 0 0.3}**

Drawn objects

Objects generated by commands like draw, pMesh, isoSurface, geoSurface, dipole or polyhedra can receive an identifier that allows referring to them in subsequent commands. That identifying name may be any combination of alphanumeric characters, as long as it does not match a command or keyword in the scripting language (it is safest to include a number in the identifier). Depending on the command, later reference to the object can be made with just that name or else must be prefixed with a dollar sign, **$**. (This will be pointed out when each command is explained.)

Scripting language - Level 1

Loading molecular models (I)

The command to load a molecular model into Jmol (that is, to read a molecular coordinate file) is **load**, followed by the filename which may optionally be placed between double quotes[1]. Any file extension is valid, since Jmol will always determine the format by reading the file contents. A list of recognized formats is shown under "Obtaining molecular models", p. 23. If you work with Jmol embedded within web pages, it is very convenient that filenames and paths follow some compatibility rules (check out "General recommendations for files" on p. 97).

Examples:

- load arginine.mol

- load ../models-prot/hemoglob.pdb.gz

- load http://biomodel.uah.es/model1/dna/140d.pdb
  (absolute paths like this will only work with the application, not the applet)

For web pages including molecular models to work from a CD-ROM, hard disk, USB disk or any other local disk, the model must be in the same folder as the applet files, or below it[2]. For pages that are read from a web server, the model must be on the same server as the page[3]. (These limitations are imposed by security restrictions of Java applets.)

It is also feasible to load models from several files, or to load just one model from a file that contains several of them; these possibilities are explained in volume 2.

Note 1: Quotes are customary if the path or filename contains a space, but in a web page environment we recommend not to use such names, for the sake of compatibility (see "General recommendations for files", p. 97).

Note 2: If you follow the method recommended in this handbook, the applet files will be at the root folder of your website, so the model files may be in any folder within the site.

Note 3: There are ways to load models located on another server, but they are described in volume 2.

Loading scripts

Among the different ways[1] to issue commands to modify the models in Jmol, one is to read a script file (that contains a series of commands for the model); the command to do so, and hence to apply the script, is **script**, followed by the filename which may optionally go between double quotes. The file must be plain text, and may have any extension[2]. It is very convenient that filenames and paths follow the rules for compatibility with the web (check out "General recommendations for files" on p. 97).

Examples:

- script **prepare.txt**

- script **scripts/spheres.spt**

- script
  http://biomodel.uah.es/model1/dna/140d_1.spt
  (absolute paths like this will only work with the
  application, not the applet)

Note 1: A description can be seen in the introductory paragraph, "Issuing commands", p. 44.

Note 2: On this handbook we will use the **spt** extension for script files (abbreviated from *script*; this extension is compulsory when preparing pages that use MDL Chime, and we keep it for Jmol due to habit and compatibility with many pre-existing scripts).

Restoring and removing the model

The **reset** command restores the model to its initial position, orientation and size, and redefines the center of rotation to be at the center of the model.

However, this does not affect the kind of rendering, colors, etc.; in order to recover the initial display characteristics of the model, you must load it again (using **load** *""*).

Another command, **initialize**, restores several options and variables of the program that may have been formerly changed.

Finally, to remove the model, leaving an empty Jmol panel, use **zap**.

Atom size

Atoms are rendered as spheres, whose radius is set using **spacefill** (synonymous: cpk).

Examples:

- spacefill on displays spheres, with van der Waals radius corresponding to each element[1] (the word on can be omitted);

- spacefill off hides the atoms (by reducing their dimension to zero); it does not affect bonds or any other renderings;

- spacefill **50%** produces spheres with half the van der Waals radius;

- spacefill **120%** produces spheres 20% bigger than van der Waals;

- spacefill **50** produces spheres with a 50/250 angstroms radius;

- spacefill **1.0** produces spheres with a 1 angstrom radius.

Note 1: Atomic and ionic radii used by Jmol can be looked up on the companion website.

Bond thickness

Bonds are rendered as cylindrical sticks, with their diameter set by **wireframe**.

Examples:

- wireframe on displays bonds as "wire frame", i.e. 1-pixel width lines (on may be omitted).

- wireframe off hides the bonds

- wireframe **30** displays sticks with a 30/250 angstroms diameter

- wireframe **0.2** displays sticks with a 0.2 angstrom diameter

Schematic styles (I)

These simplified renderings are applied to the trajectory or "backbone" of proteins (polypeptides) and nucleic acids (polynucleotides). Their advantage is to appreciate more easily the folding of the chain in space and its secondary structure. The trajectory is defined as the series of main atoms of the backbone, which are alpha carbons in a protein and phosphorus atoms in a nucleic acid. These commands have no effect on molecules that Jmol does not identify as proteins or nucleic acids; on the other hand, in general they can only be expected to work on **pdb** or **mmcif** format files, where above-mentioned atom types are identified.

Each style is achieved with a different command, and displayed independently of each other; therefore, it is possible to combine them. They are also independent of the style of atoms and bonds; if you want to avoid the excessive detail of the latter, you will need to hide them using spacefill off; wireframe off.

backbone: a zigzag line joining successive alpha carbons or phosphorus.

trace: a smooth curve[1] interpolated between alpha carbons or phosphorus.

ribbon(s): a solid, flat ribbon, following the interpolated curve.

meshRibbon(s): a ribbon made of crossing threads, following the interpolated curve.

strand(s): a ribbon made of parallel threads, following the interpolated curve.

cartoon(s): uses ribbons with an arrowhead for the alpha helix and beta strand stretches, and trace for the turns and the remainder (loops, random coil). All follow the interpolated curve.

rocket(s): uses cylinders with an arrowhead for alpha helices, straight planks with an arrowhead for beta strands, and trace for turns and the remainder. Each stretch of alpha or beta is straight.

Examples, applicable not only to trace, but to all of them:

- trace on displays it, with a default width (on may be omitted)

- trace off hides it

- trace 100 displays it, with 100/250 angstroms width

- trace 1.0 displays it, with 1 angstrom width

Using **on**, ribbons are wide on the alpha and beta stretches but narrow on the turns and the remainder. However, if a width value is given it will be equally applied to all.

Note 1: All the styles except backbone and rockets use the same curved trajectory. There are commands for modifying its precise path, as well as for setting a thickness for the ribbons (check out volume 2).

Coloring commands (I)

Atoms can get several colors that, by default, are "inherited" by bonds and other renderings. The choice to break that "inheritance" is illustrated in the level 2 section, p. 74.

The command is **color** (synonym: colour), followed by one of these:

- The recognized name of a color:
  black, white, red, green, blue, yellow, pink, cyan, brown, greenTint, ... (there is a complete list in the appendix).

- An RGB triplet (red, green, blue) in decimal or hexadecimal format:
  color [255,0,255] corresponds to magenta (red+blue)
  color [xFF00FF] is also magenta (red+blue).

- A coloring scheme:

  - **color cpk** each element gets its own color (default option);

  - **color amino** each amino acid gets its own color (bright for polar ones, dark for hydrophobic ones) [1];

  - **color shapely** another coloring scheme, that includes nucleotides [1];

  - **color structure** corresponds to secondary structure in proteins: helices in fuchsia; beta strands or sheets in yellow-orange; turns in blue; the remainder in white. In addition, DNA and RNA are colored purple and reddish [1];

- **color group** each residue takes a color from a rainbow gradient: from blue N- or 5'- to red -C or -3' [1];

- **color chain** each chain takes a color [1].

There is complete information about colors in one of the appendices.

Note 1: Only works with **pdb**, **mmcif** or equivalent files.

Atom expressions (I)

Many commands, particularly those for selection explained in the next subsection, refer to a subset of atoms in the molecule. The syntax to specify that subset is called an "atom expression". In select, restrict, hide, display and some other commands, atom expressions are used directly, as a parameter after the command; however, in other commands – those using a higher number of simultaneous parameters – each atom expression must be enclosed in parentheses. This different mode of use will be pointed out when each command in particular is described (if in doubt, it is always safe to use parentheses). For now, we will describe the most commonly used and intuitive atom expressions; those more sophisticated, as well as the detailed description of what the common ones mean, are left for volume 2.

- All atoms in the molecule: **all**

- No atoms at all: **none**

- Number identifying each atom (the sequential number or serial number): it can be just the order of atoms in the file (e.g., in **mol**, **xyz** and **cml** formats), or else be explicitly assigned in the file (e.g., in **mmcif** and **pdb** formats); the syntax is **atomNo**.

   Examples: atomNo=12   atomNo<5

- Name identifying an atom: each atom may have an alphanumeric identity. In the case of biomacromolecular files in the PDB database, these identifiers are specified within the file and follow a standard (e.g., CA for alpha carbons, CB for beta carbons, etc.). In other formats that lack such a specification, Jmol generates a name using the chemical symbol and the sequential number.

Examples: **N3   *.CB**
(the meaning of the dot and the asterisk are indicated below)

- Reference to the chemical element:

  - By its name in English: **nitrogen   carbon   oxygen**

  - By the chemical symbol, prefixed with an underscore: **_N   _C   _Fe**

  - By the atomic number (using **elemNo**): elemNo=7

  - It is also possible to specify isotopes: **deuterium tritium   _2H   _3H   _31P**

In all cases, the reference covers the whole set of atoms of that element in the model.

- Description of a certain structure, that is, formula or bond pattern, using the SMILES notation in a **substructure()** command.

  Example: **substructure("[C][C](=[O])[O]")**

- Number of model, in the case of multimodel files or having loaded several files.[1]

  Example: ***/2**   (the atoms in model number 2)

- Atoms bound to a certain set of atoms.[1]

  Example: **connected(oxygen)**   (every atom bound to an oxygen atom)

- Limit of distance to certain atoms.[1]

  Example: **within(3.0, _Cu)**   (all atoms closer than 3 Å to a copper atom)

- Belonging to a molecule (a group of covalently bound atoms) or to a model.[1]

    Example: **within(molecule,atomNo=23)**

- Belonging to one of the crystallographic unit cells (in files that include such information).[1]

    Examples: **cell=555   cell={1 1 1}**

- Belonging to sets of atoms previously defined using any atom expression.[1]

    Example: **define Q1 within(3.0, _Cu); select Q1 and not _Cu**

Note 1: Details on these commands are explained on volume 2.

Atom expressions in biomolecules

pdb and **mmcif** formats, conceived for biological macromolecules in the PDB database, include more information about each atom, such as the name and number of each residue (amino acid, nucleotide or other "group"), the chain identifier if there is more than one, and an identifier name for each atom, standardized according to rules that reflect its chemical identity and position in the residue. Jmol can use all those parameters in atom expressions (with a syntax inherited from RasMol).

The composing parts of these atom expressions, specific for biomacromolecules, are the following:

- Identifying name for an atom, specified in the file following the rules of **pdb** syntax, e.g. *CA* for alpha carbons, **NE** for epsilon-amino nitrogens, **OH1** for oxygens that are so labeled in the file. The name must be prefixed with a period, and this in turn with a residue identifier or else a wildcard (* or ?, explained on p. 62)

    Examples: ***.CB   *.HN2   Lys.NE**

- Identifier number and name for a residue; they commonly correspond to its order in the sequence (using **resNo**) and to the standard abbreviation for the amino acid or nucleotide.

  Examples: Ala Cys G T HOH HEM Ala65 A28 resNo<8 14 23-27 (this is the only case where a hyphen can be used to indicate a range)

- Identifier for a polypeptide or polynucleotide chain. This must be prefixed with a colon, and this in turn with a residue identifier or else a wildcard (* or ?)

  Example: *:B (the atoms in the chain identified as "B" in the file)

- Belonging to a chain or a sequence.

  Example: within("GGCACTT",A) (the adenylate residues that form part of the GGCACTT sequence; explained on volume 2)

- Belonging to predefined sets, such as aliphatic or aromatic amino acids, acidic or basic, polar or not, charged, cyclic, ions, solvents, prosthetic groups, types of secondary structure...

  - By residue type:
    acidic, basic, polar, neutral ... **purine, pyrimidine** ...

  - By nature of the molecule (explained below):
    protein, nucleic, dna, rna, carbohydrate, hetero, ligand, solvent, water, ions ...

  - Part of the molecule:
    backbone, sidechain

  - By secondary structure in proteins:
    helix, sheet, turn

Allocation of subsets according to the nature or part of the molecule is summarized in the following table; a more detailed description of all these predefined sets is left for volume 2.

protein	polypeptides, recognized by the presence of certain atom names in each residue		
amino	standard amino acid residues, recognized by their name		
nucleic	**dna**	polynucleotides, recognized by the presence of certain atom names in each residue	
	rna		
carbohydrate	some standard monosaccharide residues, recognized by their names		
hetero	**solvent**	**water**	water associated with the molecule, recognized by its name
		ions	free phosphate and sulphate
	ligands	all the remaining atoms (prosthetic groups, organic or inorganic ligands, ions)	
backbone	backbone of the molecule, formed by the set of atoms with certain identifying names (in proteins: carbonyl, amino, alpha carbon and their hydrogens; in nucleic acids: phosphate and pentose)		
sidechain	all atoms not qualifying as backbone		

We must remind you that all these forms of specifying subsets of atoms rely solely on the identifiers assigned to each atom in the coordinate file, and not on any chemical or structural interpretation by Jmol. For example, Jmol does not interpret a residue as alanine, it just reads whether its identifying name is ALA or, in another example, whether a carbon is identified as CA, independently of whether it truly is the alpha carbon in an amino acid. There is however some degree of structural interpretation for the keywords helix, sheet, turn, where the geometric arrangement of successive atoms identified with CA is examined in order to assign one type of secondary structure or another.

More can be specified by combining identifiers, in a precise order and with certain separator characters:

	residue or group			.	atom type	/	model no. [1]
	residue name	**residue no.**	**:chain**				
Example: **Ser70:A.CA**	**Ser**	**70**	**:A**	**.**	**CA**		
alpha carbon in serine 70 on chain A	serine	residue 70 in the sequence	chain "A"		atoms labeled "CA" (alpha carbons)		in all models
Example: **Ser70.CA**	**Ser**	**70**		**.**	**CA**		
alpha carbon in serines 70 on all chains	serine	residue 70 in the sequence	no chain speci-fied		atoms labeled "CA" (alpha carbons)		in all models
Example: **HOH.O/2**	**HOH**			**.**	**O**	**/**	**2**
oxygen atoms in water on model no. 2	water mole-cule		no chain speci-fied		oxygen atom		in model no. 2

Note 1: As will be described in volume 2, a file may contain several "models" or "frames".

Any of the parts comprising the combined identifier may be omitted, but to avoid misinterpretations it is important to retain the separators (colon, period, slash) and to fill in the gaps with wildcards. For example, CA will be interpreted as atoms belonging to residues or groups named CA and not as alpha carbons, which requires *.CA. Similarly, A is interpreted as atoms in adenylate residues, while to select chain A we need to use *:A.

These are the wildcards accepted in these identifiers:

- the asterisk * substitutes for any group of characters (or none);

- the question mark ? substitutes for a single character (or none).

Combining expressions

It is possible – and common – to combine several expressions into one; for that, we use:

- logical operators:
  and , or , not
  (a comma may be used instead of or)

- mathematical operators:
  = , == (equal to)
  < , > , <= , >= (less than, more than, less than or equal to, more than or equal to)
  <> , != , /= (different from)

- parentheses **( )**

- **selected**, **hidden** and **displayed** keywords (corresponding to the subsets of atoms affected by the most recent select, hide or display command; these are explained on the next subsection)

Examples:

- **his and nitrogen** the nitrogen atoms in histidines

- **his or nitrogen** all atoms in histidines plus all nitrogen atoms in the model

- **arg,lys** all atoms in arginine or lysine residues

- **(resNo>14 and resNo<18) and *.CA** the alpha carbons in residues 14 to 18;
in other way: **14-18 and *.CA**

- **14,16,18,20** the whole residues 14, 16, 18 and 20

- **backbone and *:B** the backbone of chain B

- **backbone and not *:B** the backbone of all chains except chain B

- **hetero and not water** the prosthetic groups except water

- **hetero and not solvent** the prosthetic groups except solvents (that is, water, phosphate and sulphate); a more simple form in this case: **ligand**

- **selected and sulphur** the sulphur atoms that belong to whatever was previously selected

- **selected or Ser** whatever was previously selected plus all atoms in serines

- **not selected** all that was not selected previously

- **carbon and not selected** carbons belonging to whatever was not previously selected

- **not hidden** whatever was not hidden

- **displayed** whatever was not hidden

- **displayed and water** whatever was not hidden plus any water molecules

Selecting part of the model

All commands that set a rendering style (size, color, schematics, labels, etc.) affect only the currently selected part of the model; initially, the whole molecule is selected. That's why it is important to be able to select those atoms whose style we want to modify.

The command to select – without yet affecting the rendering – is **select**, followed by an atom expression.

Another command, **restrict**, selects the specified part and hides the remainder.

A third one, **hide**, conceals part of the molecule without altering the selection, and its opposite, **display**, shows just part of the molecule without altering the selection.

		visualization	
		affected	not affected
selection	affected	restrict	select
	not affected	hide, display	

restrict is kept for compatibility with former versions and with RasMol and Chime, but it is advisable to avoid its use, since it is hardly reversible, as it acts by reducing to zero atom radius and bond diameter, and by suppressing schematic renderings, labels, etc., so it is difficult to recover later the previous characteristics of that part of the model that has been concealed. Instead, it is better to use **hide** which, on the contrary, acts by controlling an independent parameter, the "visibility" of each atom, and is completely reversible by using **display** (or, rather, hide none).

On the other hand, it is important to bear in mind that both **hide** and **display** apply the opposite effect to whatever part is not indicated. For example, `hide carbon` will hide carbon atoms, but at the same time will also display all the other atoms, even if they were previously hidden. In turn, `display carbon` will show all carbons and hide the rest.

In the following examples, where `select` is used, `restrict`, `hide` or `display` could be used similarly:

- Select all atoms: **select all**

- Don't select anything: **select none**

- Display all atoms: **display all** or **hide none**

- Hide all atoms: **hide all** or **display none**

- Select all atoms of a chemical element:
  select nitrogen, select sulphur ...
  select elemNo=14 ...
  select _N, select _S ...

- Select an atom based on its identifier number or serial number:
  select atomNo=14 ...

- **select selected or Ser** expands the current selection adding all serines

- **select not selected** inverts the selection

- **select carbon and not selected** selects those carbon atoms belonging to whatever was not previously selected

- **restrict selected** hides all that was not selected, keeping the selection

- **hide sidechain and selected** hides the side chains of residues that were previously selected, without altering the previous selection

- **select not hidden** selects whatever was not hidden

Assistance during selection

The currently selected part of the molecule can be checked at any moment using the pop-up menu: the **Select** entry on this menu includes – between parentheses – the number of atoms selected. Furthermore, **Select** > **Selection Halos** draws orange circles around the selected atoms. We also have **Select** > **Display Selected Only** which, obviously, hides the remainder atoms (using commands equivalent to `hide`). Finally, any time the selection changes, the new number of selected atoms is reported with a message in the console.

There are equivalent mechanisms that use the scripting language, covered in volume 2.

Hydrogen and disulphide bonds (I)

Hydrogen bonds (**hBonds**) are rendered as dashed lines or dashed sticks.

If the file specifies hydrogen bonds (possible, e.g., in **pdb** format, although infrequent), they will be displayed by using **hBonds on**; in any other case, a first call is required to **hBonds calculate**. Please note that Jmol only calculates hydrogen bonds between nitrogenous bases in a nucleic acid and between protein backbone atoms, as long as they satisfy certain distance and colinearity requirements.

Disulphide bonds (**ssBonds**) are rendered as continuous lines or sticks (similar to other covalent bonds).

Apart from that, the syntax is the same as for normal bonds (**wireframe**, p. 52); all examples here shown with ssBonds can equally be applied to hBonds:

- **hBonds calculate** calculates where H bonds are, discarding any H bond information present in the file, and displays them as thin lines (applying an implicit hBonds on).

- There is no `ssBonds calculate`

- **`ssBonds on`** displays bonds as thin lines (`on` may be omitted)

- **`ssBonds off`** hides the bonds

- **`ssBonds 25`** renders bonds as sticks, 25/250 angstroms in diameter

- **`ssBonds 0.2`** gives sticks 0.2 angstroms in diameter

Color of the Jmol panel

The background color of the Jmol panel can be changed (once generated), using **`color background`**:

- **`color background blueTint`** colors the background in a certain shade of pastel blue

- **`color background [xFFC0C0]`** ditto pale pink

Text in the Jmol panel

Two types of text can be displayed in Jmol: associated to atoms, and consequently moving with them, and static text, at fixed locations in the panel. The first case is described in the next subsection ("labels"); the second, in the level 2 section (p. 79) and in volume 2.

Labels associated with atoms (I)

Text can be placed attached to atoms, using the **`label`** command.

Examples:

- **`label on`** displays the default label, which is
  [*residue*] *number*:*chain*.*atom* #*number*
  (the `on` keyword may be omitted)

- **label off**   hides the label

- **label binding site**   labels selected atoms with the string "binding site"

- **label binding | site**   the vertical line (or "pipe" character) places the text following the "pipe" on the next line

- **label %a**   labels with the identifier name in the file for each selected atom

- **label %e**   labels with the chemical symbol of the element

- **label %i**   labels with each atom's serial number, or sequential number in the file

- **label %n**   labels with the name of the residue

- **label %r**   labels with the residue number

- **label %c**   labels with the chain's identifier

(There are more options; since they will be less frequently used, they are left for volume 2)

To control the labels appearance, check out subsections for coloring and fonts in the level 2 section (p. 74 and 78).

Axes and boxes

Bound box

Using **boundBox on** surrounds the model with a parallelogram that completely encloses the locations of all atoms; it is hidden with **boundBox off**. Only the edges are displayed, as lines whose thickness can be set with **boundBox** *number* (interpreted as pixels if integer, as angstroms if it has a decimal point), which, in addition, activates its display. The default color for these lines is either white or black, to contrast with the background, but may be set otherwise using **color boundBox** color code or name.

Coordinate axes

Atomic coordinates constituting the model belong to a Cartesian system whose axes can be displayed and hidden using **axes on** and **axes off**. With **axes** number the thickness of the axes is set (in pixels if integer, in angstroms if it contains a decimal point); in addition, their display is activated.

By default, the three axes are colored red, green and blue; the other available choice is achieved using **color axes** color code or name (then, the same color is applied to all three axes).

Note : When a crystallographic model is loaded (with fractional coordinates, based on the unit cell), the axes are displaced by default to match the edges of the unit cell, so they stop being orthogonal and stop corresponding to the atomic coordinate system. For non-crystal models, by default the axes do correspond to the model coordinate system and are orthogonal, but they are shifted to the model's center (that is, they are not placed on the atomic coordinates' origin). For more details, check out the subsection devoted to crystallographic models in volume 2.

Crystallographic unit cell

The unit cell (in models that include crystallographic information) is displayed and hidden, as a parallelogram, using **unitCell on** and **unitCell off**, respectively. Note that if the axes are active, they substitute for three of the cell edges. At the same time, text is displayed in the upper-left area of the Jmol panel, showing the unit cell parameters.

Thickness of the lines that form the edges of the unit cell is set with **unitCell** number (as usual, an integer is taken as pixels and a decimal as angstroms); when a thickness is set, the display is also activated. Their default color is either white or black, in contrast with the background, but may be set otherwise using **color unitCell** color code or name.

Scripting language - Level 2

Status variables

All the commands described up to this point are applied immediately, are independent from other commands and, when they affect the rendering style of the molecule, they apply only to the currently selected part of the model.

In contrast, there are some commands that set options that remain active until they are changed again, and in that way, affect the action of subsequent commands. To understand this, look at options like "Hydrogen atoms" (p. 40), that have a checkbox beside them in the pop-up menu: the state of that option (to show or not to show any hydrogen atoms in the model) remains activated or inactivated, affecting the result of other menu options and other commands.

All these options are internally set in Jmol by setting status variables, whose value is either true or false. In the command language, such variables are set using the **set** command. So, we will, for example, set defaultScript, set frank, set cartoonRockets, set showMultipleBonds, etc., whose companion parameter is always either **on** (activated, or **true**) or **off** (inactivated, or **false**)[1]. Default or initial values for all these variables are restored when the initialize command is used (p. 50).

The status of a variable can be checked using **show** name of the variable, and that of the whole set of variables using **set** (with nothing afterwards).

In this handbook I have chosen to present each set variant together with the command it affects, following a concept and function approach, instead of combining all set commands under the same subsection, as it is frequent on reference guides. As a consequence, in the Index of commands and keywords (p. 137) the word `set` has been omitted and the indexing term is the name of the variable.

Note 1: Some `set` commands admit a parameter other than the logical or Boolean `on/off` in order to be more easily used, but internally these are translated into Boolean parameters; for example, `set hBonds backbone` (p. 80) acts by setting the variable `hbondsBackbone = true`, while `set hBonds sidechain` acts by setting `hbondsBackbone = false`.

Loading molecular models (II)

(Check also the level 1 section, p. 49, and volume 2)

Applying a default script to all loaded models

Every model loaded into a Jmol panel may automatically receive a certain predefined script.

`set defaultLoadScript "`commands**`"`**

Example:

- **`set defaultLoadScript "spacefill off; wireframe 0.2"`**
  renders molecules as thick sticks (rather than the default, balls and thin sticks).

Default location of models

If all model files are in the same folder, this folder's path can be omitted from subsequent `load` commands. (This option applies only to the applet.)

`set defaultDirectory` folder path

Interface

The "Jmol" logo (or "frank") that is shown by default in the lower-right corner of the panel may be hidden:

`set frank off`

It is also possible to hide the name of the currently loaded molecule and its filename, which normally are shown as the topmost item in the pop-up menu and the last item in the immediate sub-menu:

`set hideNameInPopup on`

You can also inactivate the pop-up menu altogether:

`set disablePopupMenu on`

(These last two options are useful, for example, when developing assessment pages where the user is requested to identify the molecule, or if we want to prevent any change in rendering of the model.)

Finally, the user can be prevented from changing the model size (or zoom) using the mouse:

`zoom off`

(this command has two side effects: it restores the model to the starting zoom of 100%, and it delays the effect of any `zoom` command until it is reactivated with `zoom on`).

Schematic styles (II)

These are variations of the basic rendering styles described in the level 1 section (p. 52):

In `ribbons` and `cartoons`, the flat ribbons may have a thick border (inactive by default):

`set ribbonBorder on`

In `strands`, the ribbons are formed by 5 strands by default; this number can be changed (between 1 and 20):

`set strands` `number` (synonym: `set strandCount`)

An alternative rendering of `cartoons` produces ribbons for beta strand stretches but alpha helix stretches are rendered as cylinders similar to those in `rockets`:

```
set cartoonRockets on; cartoons on
```

(this variant is accessible directly from the pop-up menu, **Style > Structures > Cartoon Rockets**).

Coloring commands (II)

(Read the level 1 section before, p. 54.)

By default, the **color** command applies color to atoms, and all associated items adopt (or "inherit") that color: bonds, schematic renderings, labels. However, it is possible to set the color separately for each object and to make it independent from the color of the associated atom. Colors of objects not associated to atoms, such as text in the panel, measurements, axes, bounding box, vectors, drawn objects, surfaces, etc., can also be set.

The syntax is common:

color | *object* | *translucency* | *color or coloring scheme* |

The *object* (if not indicated, atoms is assumed) can be:

- An item representing atoms, bonds or structures:
    - **atom(s), dots, halo(s), star(s), polyhedra**
    - **bonds, hBonds, ssBonds**
    - **backbone, cartoon(s), ribbon(s), meshRibbon(s), strand(s), trace, rocket(s)**
- An item associated with atoms:
    - **label(s), hover, label background, hover background**
    - **monitor = measure(s) = measurement(s)**[1]**, rubberBand**

- An object related to the molecule as a whole, or to a Jmol panel:

    - **axes, boundBox, unitCell**

    - **vector(s)**

    - **echo, background**

- A molecular surface or a drawn object:

    - **isoSurface, geoSurface, pMesh, mo, draw**

- A chemical element [2], specified either by name in English, e.g.:
  carbon, hydrogen, nitrogen, oxygen,...
  or by its symbol prefixed with an underscore, e.g.:
  _C, _H, _N, _O;
  isotopes are also included:
  deuterium, tritium, _2H, _3H, _31P, ...

- The name given to an object when it is generated by **draw, isosurface, pmesh** or **polyhedra**, prefixed with a dollar sign, **$**.

The *translucency* term can be

- **opaque** (default option): opaque surfaces are used for the atom spheres, the bond cylinders, the schematic renderings...

- **translucent**: semitransparent surfaces are used instead. (Most recent versions of Jmol include several levels of translucency; check out volume 2.)

  Both may be applied alone, or preceding any of the color settings. If none is indicated, opaque is assumed.

The *color or coloring scheme* may be

- A recognized color name: black, blue, brown, etc. (there is a complete list in one of the appendices)

- A decimal [*red*, *green*, *blue*] or hexadecimal [x*RRGGBB*] triplet. Examples: [176,255,0] or [xB0FF00] both give a yellowish green shade

- A recognized coloring scheme: alt, amino, chain, charge, formalCharge, partialCharge, cpk, group, monomer, model, shapely, structure, temperature, fixedTemperature or relativeTemperature
(there are more details in the color appendix)

  - Coloring schemes cannot be applied to bonds, hBonds, ssBonds, axes, echo, hover, isoSurface, measure(ment), monitor, pMesh, unitCell, nor to the chemical elements (however, bonds, hBonds, ssBonds can acquire coloring schemes by inheritance from atoms).

  - Both group and monomer color residues according to their position along a macromolecular chain: from N- or 5'- blue, to -C or -3' red.

  - group is based on the residue number and on the chain identifier, both present in the **pdb** file.

  - monomer interprets bonds between residues, using the position of the residue relative to the polymer; for example, an interrupted chain is recognized as two polymers, so they are colored independently if monomer is used.

  - formalCharge indicates the formal charge, always an integer; it is the same as charge.

- partialCharge is the partial charge, for example, calculated; it is a non-integer number.

- relativeTemperature is the same as temperature

- The keyword **type** may be used only for color hBonds, and will color them according to the distance between the amino acid residues that are bonded, measured along the protein backbone: -4=green, -3=cyan, +2=white, +3=magenta (turns), +4=red (alpha helix), +5=orange, other=yellow (beta strand). Requires a previous hBonds on.

- The keywords **none** or **inherit**, both indicating that the referred item will get the default color or that of the atom it is associated with.

Examples:

By default, hydrogen bonds are colored half and half according to the color of the atoms bonded; to choose another color for the whole bond:

- **color hBonds yellow** colors bonds in yellow

- **color hBonds [x00FF00]** colors bonds in green

- **color hBonds none** or
  color hBonds inherit the bond recovers the colors of the connected atoms

Default color for the text in a label is that of the atom. To choose another:

- **color label yellow** colors the labels (present and future) attached to the currently selected atoms in yellow.

- **color label [x00FFFF]** colors labels cyan

- **color label none** or
  color label inherit the label recovers the color of the respective atom.

Note 1: color measures affects those monitor lines defined afterwards, as well as the former ones that had no explicitly set color. color measures off may be needed to cancel previous commands and be able to apply new colors.

Note 2: When a chemical element is specified (either by name or symbol), its default color is changed (both for the current molecule and any others loaded later in that same Jmol panel). To recover the default coloring, use **set defaultColors Jmol**. You can see the default colors for each element in one of the appendices and on the back cover.

Font commands

The font (type of lettering), its size and style for each text item (echo, label, hover) is controlled with the **font** command. (Color of text is set separately, using the color command.) You can specify only the size, but in order to set the font or the style they must be preceded by a size.

- **font echo 22** uses a 22-pixel high font (approximately)

- **font echo 18 serif**

- **font echo 26 sansSerif bold**

These are the recognized keywords: **serif** (similar to Times) and **monospaced** (like Courier); any other is interpreted as **sansSerif** (Arial or Helvetica).

For the style, one of these may be added: **plain**, **bold**, **italic** or **boldItalic**.

Rendering of multiple bonds

Some coordinate file formats include the bond order (partial, single, partially double, aromatic, double, triple). On others – such as **pdb** – a similar effect can be achieved by setting the connections for each double bond twice. In any case, Jmol recognizes both situations and it can be directed to show them or not as multiple sticks.

set showMultipleBonds on displays multiple sticks

set showMultipleBonds off displays all bonds as single (except for hydrogen bonds, that remain as dashed lines or sticks)

Note : For the time being the old, RasMol- and Chime-compatible, command set bonds on/off is still supported.

Static text in the Jmol panel (I)

Static text, always displayed in front of the model, can be placed at 3 locations: top, middle and bottom and, for each of them, in one of 3 alignments: left, center or right. (To place text at other locations, see volume 2.)

The commands are **echo** and **set echo**.

First it is compulsory to define the position of the text (if this is not done, the text will not be displayed):

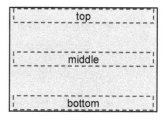

- **set echo top center**

- **set echo middle right**

- **set echo bottom left**

and then, the text string is indicated:

- **echo** lysozyme displays the text "lysozyme"

- **echo** deletes the latest text

- **set echo off** deletes all text (and prevents any other from being displayed until another of the aforementioned set echo options is again activated).

Default color for echo texts is red; to choose another:

- **color echo yellow** colors the text displayed in the position set by the most recent set echo command in yellow. (Can be applied before or after the echo command.)

You may also set the font (check out font echo in the relevant subsection, on this same level 2, p.78).

Hydrogen bonds and disulphide bonds (II)

Hydrogen bonds (hBonds) and disulphide bonds (ssBonds) extend by default between the respective atoms (O and N, N and N, S and S). However, when the atoms are not shown, as happens when using schematic backbone renderings, such bonds seem to be "hanging in empty space", and it may be visually more convenient to have them extending up to the polypeptide or polynucleotide backbone. To achieve this, we use

- **set hBonds backbone** (bonds extend to alpha carbon or phosphorus atoms)

- **set ssBonds backbone** (bonds extend to alpha carbons in cysteines)

The default option is recovered with

- **set hBonds sidechain**

- **set ssBonds sidechain**

Orientation of the model

Some commands are available for specifying a movement relative to a starting position, while others specify movement to an absolute position, independent of the previous position. On the other hand, some commands change position and orientation of the model instantly, while others do so through a smooth movement along a certain period of time.

The following table summarizes these characteristics, comparatively for all commands related to orientation or movement. Then, each one of them is analyzed in more detail.

		relative or absolute	*instantaneous or progressive*
Just rotation:	`rotate`	R	I
	`spin`	R	P
Just translation:	`translate`	A	I
Just size change:	`zoom`	R / A	I
	`zoomTo`	R / A	I / P
Rotation, translation and size change:	`move`	R	I / P
	`moveTo`	A	I / P
Change in the rotation center:	`center`, with previous `setWindowCentered off`	(R)	I
Change in the rotation center and size change:	`zoom`, with previous `setWindowCentered off`	R	I
	`zoomTo`, with previous `setWindowCentered off`	A	I / P
Change in the rotation center, size change and translation to the center:	`center`, with previous `setWindowCentered on`	A	I
	`zoom`, with previous `setWindowCentered on`	A	I
	`zoomTo`, with previous `setWindowCentered on`	A	I / P

Rotation (I)

The molecule can rotate around the 3 "external" axes, anchored to the panel, or around "internal" axes, associated to the model. The default rotation center is the geometric center of the molecule. Instantaneous rotation to reorient the molecule is done with **rotate**, while a permanent rotation over time is the consequence of **spin**. These two commands use the same syntax.

(Only the most frequent possibilities are explained here; others are described on volume 2.)

spin on starts the rotation, or spinning, as specified in a previous spin command; **spin off** stops any rotation.

a) Rotation around an external axis

This refers to the axes fixed onto the Jmol panel: X horizontal, Y vertical, Z perpendicular to screen [1].

rotate | *rotation axis: X, Y or Z* | *angle* |

spin | *rotation axis: X, Y or Z* | *speed* |

Angle is set in sexagesimal degrees and speed in degrees per second. Examples:

- rotate x **45**
- rotate z **-15**
- spin y **-10**

Rotation around a non-Cartesian axis can be achieved by defining it between the center of the panel and a given point (in panel, or external, coordinates):

rotate axisAngle { *coordinates* **}** *angle*

spin axisAngle { *coordinates* **}** *speed*

Example:

- spin axisAngle **{1 1 0} 30** spins around an axis positioned at 45° (bisecting XY), at 30°/s

Note 1: Axes orientation in Jmol is different to that in RasMol 2.6 and in Chime, hence the effect of `rotate` and `spin` commands may be opposite. To get the same orientation, where RasMol and Chime use `rotate z`, for Jmol the angle value must change sign.

	RasMol (up to 2.6) and Chime	*Jmol*
positive direction of X	to the right	to the right
positive direction of Y	down	up
positive direction of Z	back	front
positive X rotation	counterclockwise	counterclockwise
positive Y rotation	clockwise	counterclockwise
positive Z rotation	counterclockwise	counterclockwise

b) Rotation around an internal axis

In this case, the X, Y, Z axes used are those belonging to the coordinate system of the model which, therefore, rotate and translate with it. (These axes can be shown using `axes on`)

rotate molecular $\boxed{X, Y \text{ or } Z}$ $\boxed{angle}$

spin molecular $\boxed{X, Y \text{ or } Z}$ $\boxed{speed}$

A non-Cartesian axis can also be used, in this case defined by two points:

rotate $\boxed{point\ 1}$ $\boxed{point\ 2}$ $\boxed{angle}$

spin $\boxed{point\ 1}$ $\boxed{point\ 2}$ $\boxed{speed}$

For these latter two forms, the keyword `molecular` is implicit. The reference *points* may be

- $\{\boxed{x}\ \boxed{y}\ \boxed{z}\}$ an internal, model-based coordinate, enclosed in braces;

- $\{\boxed{a/b}\ \boxed{c/d}\ \boxed{e/f}\}$ a fractional (crystallographic) internal coordinate, enclosed in braces;

- $(\boxed{atom\ expression})$ the center of an atom or group of atoms, specified between parentheses;

- $\$\boxed{object\ name}$ the center of an object previously drawn using the **draw** command, its name prefixed with the dollar sign, $.

Examples:

- `rotate molecular z` **30** rotates 30° around the model's internal Z axis

- `spin {1.0 -0.6 0} {2.3 1.1 0.5}` **-15** rotates 15° per second, in the opposite direction, around the axis defined by the points (1,-0.6,0) and (2.3,1.1,0.5), in internal coordinates

- `spin (atomNo=11) (atomNo=14)` **-20** rotates 20° per second around the axis defined by atoms with sequential numbers 11 and 14

Translation

The molecule can be moved – instantly – along the X (horizontal) and Y (vertical) axes using `translate` command. Translation along Z axis is equivalent to moving the model closer or further away, or a change in its apparent size, and hence corresponds to `zoom`, described in the next subsection.

`translate` *direction: X or Y* *position*

position (an integer) is measured with respect to a fixed reference system, where the center of the Jmol panel is (0, 0) and its dimensions are 100. Therefore, `translate x` **50** moves the molecule to the right so that its center rests on the right-hand edge of the panel.

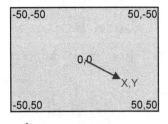

It is important to assimilate that translation is not relative, but absolute: we indicate not how much the model will move with respect to its current position, but rather the position it will reach with respect to the fixed reference system, irrespective of its previous position.

Note: Axes orientation in Jmol is different to that in RasMol 2.6 and in Chime (see table on previous note), hence the effect of `translate` command may be opposite. To get the same position, where RasMol and Chime use `translate` y, for Jmol the translation value must change sign.

Size

The observed apparent size of the molecule is conceptually equivalent to the distance between it and the observer, and is defined initially as 100%; upon file loading, the model automatically fits so that, in spacefill mode, it fills all space available in the panel (if this is rectangular in shape, it is convenient to use `set zoomLarge`, described next).

a) Absolute change

The abovementioned size can be modified instantly with **zoom** command, or gradually over a certain time using **zoomTo**:

zoom `size`

zoomTo `time` `size`

The *size* value is interpreted as a percentage relative to the starting size, i.e. to panel dimensions. The *time* involved in the change is set in seconds (it can be omitted, and will be one second by default). So:

- **zoom** 100 restores the initial molecule size
- **zoom** 30 the molecule will take up 30% of the panel dimensions
- **zoomTo** 0.5 400 changes the size to be 4 times larger than the starting one, gradually over half a second

In this syntax (similarly to what happens with `translate`) the previous size of the model is irrelevant.

b) Relative change

It is also possible to impose a change relative to the current size:

- **zoom** *2 doubles the size
- **zoomTo** 0.5 *3 increases the size 3-fold, over half a second

- **zoom** /2 reduces the size by half

- **zoom** +20 enlarges the view, adding 20 to the current absolute value of zoom (scarcely useful, since the observable magnitude of its effect depends on the previous value: from 100 to 120 is a significant change, while from 500 to 520 is a small one)

- **zoom** -25 subtracts 25 from the current value (ditto)

c) Combination with centering

Finally, in order to focus on a certain group of atoms, we can center the model on them and apply a size, using

zoom (*atom expression*) *size*

zoomTo *time* (*atom expression*) *size*

The atom expression that defines the group of atoms must be enclosed in parentheses. The effect of this command is multiple: the geometric center of the group becomes the new center of rotation for the model; the molecule is moved so that this new center is positioned at the center of the panel[1]; the size (zoom) is adjusted according to the value provided.

As a special case, if given *size* is zero, the scale will be set so that the atom group in spacefill fills the whole panel (irrespective of the previous size).

Example:

- zoomTo **0.5** (ligand) ***4** centers the model on the non-protein groups, zooming in 4-fold, and performs all this gradually along half a second

- zoomTo **2** (ligand) **0** centers the model on the non-protein groups, enlarging them as much as possible without putting them out of the panel, and performs all this gradually along 2 seconds

Note 1: This translation to the center may be avoided by previously using set windowCentered off, a command explained next.

d) Blocking

To prevent the user from changing the size (zoom) of the model with the mouse or the menu, we can employ

`zoom off`

Note, however, that this will also apply `zoom 100` and will prevent other instances of `zoom` or `zoomTo` from having a visible effect. (Their effects are remembered and will be applied when zoom is reactivated using `zoom on`; the blocking also affects zoom actions issued from the menu.)

e) Fitting rectangular panels

When a file is loaded, the model is set to a scale so that it fits within the panel in spacefill rendering at any angle of rotation. If the Jmol panel is rectangular, this fit may be done according to either the short or the long dimension.

`set zoomLarge on` fits the model to the longest dimension of the panel

`set zoomLarge off` fits the model to the shortest dimension

Note : The default value of this parameter has suffered changes during Jmol development; on v.11.2 the longest dimension is used for fitting. In anticipation of possible changes in future versions, it is convenient to set it explicitly.

Centering

The model is initially positioned with its geometric center on the panel's center, and rotates around that point. We can specify another point of the model to become the center of rotation and to move, or not, to the panel's center.

`set windowCentered on` (default option). After setting this option, any centering command (`center`, `zoom`, `zoomTo`) will move the model so that the new rotation center is located on the panel's center. Note that, usually, changing the center of a molecule will adjust its apparent size so that it fits within the panel while rotating, but the nominal `zoom` value does not change (that is, the size that corresponds to `zoom 100` is redefined).

set windowCentered off   After setting this option, any centering command will not move the model, it will just change the center of rotation. There is no forced resizing then.

center `atom expression`   (synonym: `centre`). The geometric center of the specified group of atoms becomes the new rotation center. (There will or will not be movement depending on the current value of `set windowCentered`.) The atom expression may be enclosed in parentheses, but this is not necessary.

center {`X Y Z coordinates`}   The point specified becomes the new center of rotation. The coordinates (internal to the model) must be enclosed in braces and may be separated by spaces or commas.

Examples:

- `center` or `center all`   restore the original center (the geometric center of the whole model).

- `center atomNo=`**14**   the atom with identifier 14 becomes the new center of rotation. In addition, it is moved to the panel's center and the size is readjusted so that the molecule fits completely while being rotated, except if a former `set windowCentered off` has been issued.

- `center _Fe`   the geometric average point of all iron atoms in the molecule becomes the new center of rotation (the same conditions described above apply).

- `center {`**110**`}`   the 1,1,0 point (angstroms) becomes the new center of rotation. Note that, depending on the atomic coordinates of the model, such a point may be far away from it.

Combined movement

Using the **move** and **moveTo** commands combines translation, rotation and size change, either instantly or over a certain period of time. The basic difference between these commands is that the first one produces a reorientation relative to the starting position, while the second leads to a final orientation irrespective of the starting position (in other words, they apply relative and absolute movements, respectively). The parameters given with move are easy to understand in terms of rotation and translation, while those used in moveTo are difficult to interpret and nearly always are just copied from those provided by Jmol after orienting the model manually as desired.

move | *rotX* | *rotY* | *rotZ* | *zoom* | *dX* | *dY* | *dZ* | *slab* | *time*

parameter	description	
rotX	rotation around X axis	
rotY	rotation around Y axis	
rotZ	rotation around Z axis	the given values are the relative changes that the model will undergo over the whole movement
zoom	apparent size (closer/farther), or zoom in/zoom out	
dX	translation along X	
dY	translation along Y	
dZ	translation along Z	
slab	shift of the slabbing plane (see the subsection devoted to slabbing through the model, in volume 2)	
time	total time involved in the movement (in seconds)	

Examples:

- `move` **90 0 0 0 0 0 0 0 1** rotates the model by 90° around the X axis, same as `rotate x` **90** would do but using a gradual movement along one second.

- `move` **0 720 0 0 0 0 0 0 1** rotates the model by two full turns around the Y axis, using a gradual movement along one second.

- `move` **0 0 0 0 0 25 0 0 0.5** moves the model down by 25% of the panel's height, with a gradual movement along half a second. (The final position is not necessarily the same as with `translate y` **25**, since this latter is an absolute position, while with `move` it is relative to the starting position.)

- `move` **90 15 0 100 0 20 0 0 2** over a 2 second time period, the model rotates by 90° around the X axis and 15° around the Y axis, increases its size by adding 100 to the zoom value and is translated down by 20% of the panel's height (not in that order, rather, all at the same time).

Note : In order to adapt Chime scripts for Jmol, these changes must be made: move x y -z * x -y -z * * * *

With **moveTo**, the resulting orientation is not relative to the previous one, but to that of the molecule when it was loaded; that is to say, if the same `moveTo` command is issued a second time, the orientation of the molecule is not altered further. Although the meaning of the parameters in the `moveTo` command can be described, their comprehension and their manual choice are not simple, and from a practical pint of view they are only used as provided by the software from a manually achieved orientation.

The most common way of using moveTo is:

1. reposition the molecule using the mouse and commands in the console, until you get the desired orientation and size;

2. open the pop-up menu and choose **Show > Orientation**;

3. on the **Script Console** the moveTo command that reproduces the current orientation will be shown; highlight it with the mouse and copy it (**Ctrl+C**);

4. paste that command into the page or the script file from which you want it to be used.

The same result is obtained by typing **show orientation** in the console, rather than using the menu.

Note that the result shown on the console consists of two equivalent commands: one uses moveTo, the other reset, center, rotate and translate. You can use either of them; we suggest moveTo. Example:

	$ show orientation
This is the useful part:	moveto /* time, axisAngle */ **1.0** { -927 -300 225 165.15} /* zoom, translation */ 100.0 0.08 0.0 /* center, rotationRadius */ {3.5825 -2.2215 1.819} 10.259438 /* navigation center, translation, depth */ {0.0 0.0 0.0} -3.0926816 24.158844 50.0;
	OR #Follows Z-Y-Z convention for Euler angles reset;center {3.5825 -2.2215 1.819}; rotate z -48.02; rotate y 150.13; rotate z 167.84 translate x 0.08; rotationRadius = 10.26; Script completed

The only change you may need on this command is the time period used for the movement, which by default is set to one second; it is the first numerical value in the `moveTo` command (highlighted in bold type on the above example).

Measurements

Since model visualization software works with each atom's coordinates, it is trivial for it to provide measurements of distance and angles. In Jmol, this is achieved with **measure** and **set measure** commands (in both, `measure` takes several synonyms: `measures`, `measurement`, `measurements`, `monitor`, `monitors`). These work by drawing a "monitor" line between the chosen atoms and attaching to it a text label with the measurement. Distance measurements can be expressed in nanometers, angstroms, picometers (10^{-9}, 10^{-10} and 10^{-12} m, respectively) or in Bohr atomic units (1 Bohr $\cong 5.3\times10^{-11}$ m = 0.53 Å). Angle measurements are always expressed in sexagesimal degrees. In addition, it is possible to hide the measurement label and leave only the line.

a) Monitor lines

To specify on which atoms we want a monitor line (its display and its measurement label are automatically activated):

measure `no. of atom` `no. of atom` to measure a distance

measure `no. of atom` `no. of atom` `no. of atom` to measure an angle

measure `no. of atom` `no. of atom` `no. of atom` `no. of atom` to measure a dihedral angle (or torsion angle)[1]

The *no. of atom* parameter is the identifier in the coordinates file (in its absence, the order or serial number, depending on the file format). This is one of the few commands in Jmol, if not the only one, where the identifier number for an atom can be used without preceding it with `atomNo=`.

Examples:

- **measure 11 14** marks and measures a distance

- **measure 11 14 25** marks and measures an angle

- **measure 11 14 25 10** marks and measures a dihedral angle

By using atom expressions instead of identifier numbers, it is possible to generate several measurements at the same time, and more choices are available:

measure all (*atom expression* **)** ...
using 2, 3 or 4 atom expressions to measure distance, angle or torsion; each one enclosed in parentheses. This sets measurements among all atoms in the first expression and all atoms in the second, etc. (Use this variant carefully, since it may easily generate too many monitor lines.)

measure allConnected (*atom expression* **)** ...
restricts measurements to those atoms that are bonded.

Examples:

- **measure all (_Zn) (_S)**   marks and measures all distances between zinc and sulphur atoms

- **measure allConnected (_H) (_N) (_H)**   marks and measures all H-N-H angles in amino groups

To control display of monitor lines (and their associated measurements):

measure off   hides all of them

measure on   displays them again

measure delete suppresses them all, without any chance to display them again (other than defining them again)

measure delete *n*   deletes only one (with the number corresponding to the order in which they were created). It can also be done by defining it again with `measure` $\boxed{n}$ $\boxed{n}$ $\boxed{n}$ $\boxed{n}$ (atom identifier numbers).

Monitor lines are by default dotted and thin, but they can be made continuous and with a certain thickness:

set measure $\boxed{thickness}$ An integer is interpreted as pixels; a decimal, as angstroms (must be <2.0).

set measure dotted (thin and dotted, default option)

Color of both the lines and measurement labels is white or black (whatever contrasts with the background color), unless another is specified with:

color measure $\boxed{color\ name\ or\ code}$ (check out the coloring commands subsection, within this level 2 section, p. 74)

Note 1: Two atoms define a distance between their centers; 3 atoms define an angle with vertex on the second atom; 4 atoms define a dihedral angle or torsion angle, which is the angle formed between the plane defined by atoms 1, 2 and 3 and the plane defined by atoms 2, 3 and 4.

b) Measurements

Display of measurements whenever the monitor lines are displayed is controlled with

set measure on (default)

set measure off

To set the units used for distance measurements:

set measure nm

set measure pm

set measure angstroms

set measure au (Bohr atomic units)

To set the font to be used in measurement labels:

font measure $\boxed{size}$ $\boxed{font}$ $\boxed{style}$ (see font commands subsection, p. 78)

You may also specify a format for the measurements (such as number of decimals, or to include another text or the atom names...), to restrict them to certain intervals, to manage them in multimodel files, etc.; to avoid complicating the description, these options are left for a more advanced section in volume 2.

Vibration of the molecule

Some file formats include information on the vibrational modes of the molecule[1]. Jmol can display direction and amplitude of each atom's vibration using arrows (vectors) and through animation of the model.

vector **on** displays vectors

vector **off** hides them

vector |*thickness*| an integer is interpreted as a diameter for the arrow, in pixels (from 1 to 19); if it's a decimal, as a radius in angstroms (maximum 3.0)

vector **scale** |*number between -10 and 10*| sets the scale for all vectors (initially it is 1)

vibration **on** activates animation

vibration **off** stops animation

vibration |*period*| sets the rate of the animation; the *period* value gives the length (seconds) of a full vibration; the lower the period, the faster the animation

vibration **scale** |*number between -10 and 10*| sets the amplitude of all vibrations (initially it is 1)

Some of these actions can be done quickly from the pop-up menu or from the toolbar:

- Vibration menu entry, available when the file holds such information, starts and stops the animated vibration, as well as controls the display and look of the vectors.

- When the file contains the different vibrational modes of the molecule, each resonance frequency is stored in a separate model, hence the **Model** menu is also needed to see all of them; further, the menu entry itself includes their identification, which usually indicates the associated frequency. For rapid switching between models, the toolbar at the top of the application includes button controls to move forward and backward along the models, that is, through the frequencies.

Note 1: For example, **xyz** format may indicate, on columns 6 to 8 in the line corresponding to each atom, its movement along x, y, z; Gaussian format may include the harmonic frequencies. Usually each vibration mode is stored in a model or frame (generating a multimodel file, described on volume 2).

Including Jmol models in a web page - Level 1

(Before starting this section, it is helpful to have read the introductory subsections, particularly "Preparation for using the JmolApplet", p. 21.)

To insert a Jmol applet as part of the content of a web page, you must use the <APPLET> or <OBJECT> tags from HTML language. However, this is not necessary for the method recommended here, since the task is performed by the **Jmol.js** library, included in the Jmol package. Under its instructions, the browser will insert (embed) a panel or applet area, will load first Java and then the Jmol applet and, finally, will load and display a molecular model inside the panel, according to any commands that may have been provided.

On separate sections we have described in detail the numerous commands accepted by Jmol for setting the orientation, features, movement, etc. of the model. It is advisable that you work with those sections during the development of your own materials, in parallel with reading the present section and those following (levels 2 or intermediate and 3 or advanced for including models in web pages).

General recommendations for files

These recommendations, that apply both to web page (**html, gif, jpg, js, css**...), molecular coordinate and script files, are directed toward creating web pages (with Jmol molecular models) that are "portable", that is, that work correctly both in local mode and through the internet, and being visited from any kind of computer and operating system. It is advisable to follow them from the very beginning of your design of material, to avoid having to go back later and make many changes on already finished files.

1. File names should be completely lowercase, without any spaces or non-English characters (i.e., just basic ASCII, not extended; you should avoid accents, characters like ñ or ç and any kind of symbol). You can safely use numbers, standard dash or hyphen (-) and the underscore (_).[1]

2. File paths should follow the same rule and not be absolute, but relative to the folder where the web page is located.

Examples of not recommended file names and paths:	Examples of recommended file names and paths:
Réaction.htm	reaction.htm
Oleic Acid.mol	oleic-acid.mol
molécules/adénine.mol	molecules/adenine.mol
c:/molecules/insulin.pdb	../molecules/insulin.pdb

3. Organizing files into folders may be done following any criterion, obviously as long as the proper path is indicated when referencing them. One precaution is needed, though: locate the molecular coordinate files in the same folder as the Jmol files or below that folder in the tree structure. For this reason, we recommend that you locate the Jmol files in the root folder of the website; this way, the contents of the web pages (html text, images, etc.) and the models (coordinate files, script files) may be located in any arrangement you desire.

Note 1: Strictly speaking, the use of uppercase is possible, but it is discouraged here because it is a major cause of trouble when you start working on web edition. This is due to the Windows operating system not differentiating between upper- and lowercase for file names (if you want to verify this, try to create two files named **test.txt** and **Test.txt** in the same folder), while Linux, a common operating system in web servers, does indeed differentiate between both; as a consequence, links and commands that work properly on the PC fail when they are taken to the server. Experience shows that it is more efficient to get used to avoiding uppercase right from the beginning.

Jmol initialization

Each HTML page that includes molecular models, or controls that act on them, must contain a call to use the JavaScript library associated with Jmol (**Jmol.js**); such call must be within the head section of the web page (<head> tag in HTML source code):

```
<script type="text/javascript"
src="file path for Jmol.js/Jmol.js">
</script>
```

Similarly, just after starting the body of the web page (section <body> in HTML source code) this command must be included:

```
<script type="text/javascript">
jmolInitialize("file path for JmolApplet0.jar/")
</script>
```

Note :   Strictly speaking, there is no need to locate this command right at the beginning of the body; and it is sufficient just to put it before using any of the functions from **Jmol.js** library (such as `jmolApplet`, `jmolButton`, etc.); the advice to put it at the very beginning is only to avoid an oversight and prevent possible failures due to future changes in the distribution of contents of the page.

As always happens with JavaScript code, it is essential not to alter uppercase, lowercase, punctuation signs, quotes, etc., or else the page will not work.

Examples:

With this file and folder setup:

📁 **webs**
├─ 🗎 **Jmol.js**
├─ 🗎 **JmolApplet0.jar**
├─ 🗎 **JmolApplet0_Core.jar**
├─ **(etc.)**
└─ 🗎 **index.html**

the contents of **index.html** should be:

```
<head>
<script type="text/javascript" src="./Jmol.js">
</script>
</head>

<body>
<script
type="text/javascript">jmolInitialize("./")
</script>
(...)
</body>
```

And with this other arrangement:

📁 **webs**
├─ 🗎 **Jmol.js**
├─ 🗎 **JmolApplet0.jar**
├─ 🗎 **JmolApplet0_Core.jar**
├─ **(etc.)**
└─ 📁 **chap1**
    └─ 🗎 **index.html**

the contents of **index.html** should be:

```
<head>
<script type="text/javascript" src="../Jmol.js">
</script>
</head>

<body>
<script
type="text/javascript">jmolInitialize("../")
</script>
(...)
</body>
```

Inserting the model

To include a panel with the molecular model within the page (in technical terms, to embed the **JmolApplet**) the following code must be inserted at the desired place in the page:

```
<script type="text/javascript">
jmolApplet(dimensions, "commands")
</script>
```

where *dimensions* is the size in pixels of the area occupied by the model, i.e. the Jmol panel (with the same width and height; if you want a rectangular panel, it can be done with a slight modification, described in level 2, p. 110) and the – optional – *commands* dictate the loading of a model and modification of its rendering.

For example: `jmolApplet(150, "load atp.pdb")` includes in the web page a model like this:
(obviously, not a static image as here, but a model that can be rotated, moved and modified in multiple ways).

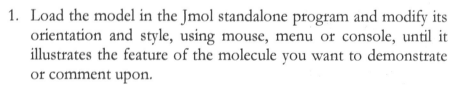

(Expansions of this command can be seen on levels 2 and 3, p. 110 and 117)

An example of simple use, where a web page displays a model with a style prepared in advance, would be the following:

1. Load the model in the Jmol standalone program and modify its orientation and style, using mouse, menu or console, until it illustrates the feature of the molecule you want to demonstrate or comment upon.

2. Save that "view" of the model to a script file, using on the top menu **File > Export > Image or script** and choosing SPT format (a script of commands). Let's suppose you call the file **view-1.spt**

3. Locate the file in a folder that forms part of the set of your web pages (for example, the same folder where you have **JmolApplet** files, or else in a subfolder below this).

4. In the source code of the web page you are building, insert the command:

```
<script type="text/javascript">
jmolApplet(200, "script view-1.spt")
</script>
```

Handling the model with simple controls: buttons, links and checkboxes

Models located in a web page can be controlled from hyperlinks, buttons or other types of controls placed in the page itself, that will apply a series of Jmol commands (the available commands are described in other sections of this handbook). Such series are called scripts or macros.

The controls most easy to program are buttons than can be pushed (clicked), hyperlinks and checkboxes (which allow a checked state ☑ and an unchecked one ☐). To place one of these Jmol controls in the page you must insert, respectively, one of these pieces of code:

Buttons

For a clickable button:

```
<script type="text/javascript">
jmolButton("commands", "text displayed")
</script>
```

Example:

```
<script type="text/javascript">
jmolButton("spacefill on", "spheres model")
</script>
```

The result is: [spheres model]. When the button is clicked, the command `spacefill on` will be applied to the model (rendering the atoms as spheres with their van der Waals radii).

Links

For a hyperlink:

```
<script type="text/javascript">
jmolLink("commands", "text displayed")
</script>
```

Example:

```
<script type="text/javascript">
jmolLink("spacefill on", " spheres model")
</script>
```

The result is: spheres model. When the link is clicked, the command `spacefill on` will be applied to the model.

Checkboxes

For a checkbox:

```
<script type="text/javascript">
jmolCheckbox("commands when checked",
"commands when unchecked", "text displayed")
</script>
```

Example:

```
<script type="text/javascript">
jmolCheckbox("spacefill on", "spacefill off", "spheres
model")
</script>
```

The result is: □spheres model. When the checkbox is checked, the command `spacefill on` will be applied; when it is unchecked, the command `spacefill off` will be applied.

Including Jmol models in a web page - Level 2

Handling the model with combined controls: radio buttons and menus

The models may be also controlled from radio buttons, that is, mutually exclusive options, or using menus, pull-down lists whose options are also mutually exclusive.

To use these, first a JavaScript data array must be defined; each of its elements is in itself another array with a script, a text and optionally a flag for the button to be initially checked, or the menu option to be initially selected.

Radio buttons

For a group of radio buttons:

```
<script type="text/javascript">
var x = new Array()
```
(any other name may be used in place of x)

Each element of the array, x[0], x[1] etc. must consist of:

```
x[j] = ["commands", "text displayed",
true or false flag]
jmolRadioGroup(x, "separator between options")
</script>
```

Example:
```
<script type="text/javascript">
var x = new Array()
x[0] = ["spacefill off; wireframe on", "Wireframe"]
x[1] = ["spacefill 20%; wireframe 40", "Balls and sticks ",
true]
x[2] = ["spacefill 100%; wireframe off", "Spheres"]
```

```
jmolRadioGroup(x, "<br>")
</script>
```

      ○ Wireframe
      ◉ Balls and sticks
The result is: ○ Spheres   . Whenever an option is checked, the others get unchecked and the corresponding script of commands is applied to the model. Initially, the second radio button is checked (since it is x[1] which has the "true" value in the third place).

The *separator between options* is HTML text that will be inserted between every two consecutive radio buttons. For example, "<br>" for a line break, " " for a space, " " for a non-breaking space.

Menus

For a pull-down menu or list, the format is very similar:

```
<script type="text/javascript">
var x = new Array()
```
    (any other name may be used instead of x)
Each element of the array, x[0], x[1] etc. must consist of:
```
x[j] = ["commands", "text displayed",
true or false flag]
jmolMenu(x)
</script>
```

(In a menu, a separator is not used)

Example:

```
<script type="text/javascript">
var x = new Array()
x[0] = ["spacefill off; wireframe on", "Wireframe"]
x[1] = ["spacefill 20%; wireframe 40", "Balls and sticks",
true]
```

```
x[2] = ["spacefill 100%; wireframe off", "Spheres"]
jmolMenu(x)
</script>
```

The result is: . When an item from the menu is chosen, the matching commands are applied to the model. Initially the second item is selected.

Handling the model based on JavaScript events (I)

It is equally possible to pass commands to the model directly as a consequence of JavaScript events not associated with a form-type control – as are the already shown buttons, checkboxes, radio buttons and menus.

```
<script type="text/javascript">
jmolScript("commands")
</script>
```

Example:

```
<script type="text/javascript">
jmolScript("spacefill off; wireframe on")
</script>
```

The result is: the commands are applied to the model when that section of the JavaScript code is activated (it may be part of the page, of an event like onLoad or onClick, of a JavaScript function, …).

Warning: while the commands are being applied to the model, execution of JavaScript and HTML code continues in parallel. For example, if we use

```
<script type="text/javascript">
jmolScript ("load hemoglobin.pdb")
alert ("the model has been loaded")
</script>
```

The alert dialog will show up before the model has had time to load.

Or, if we use

```
<script type="text/javascript">
jmolScript ("load hemoglobin.pdb")
jmolScript ("color amino")
</script>
```

The coloring command will likely fail because the model has not been loaded yet.

To avoid this, a command is available that delays execution of other processes until the current one has finished executing:

```
<script type="text/javascript">
jmolScriptWait (" commands ")
</script>
```

In addition, both this command and the related jmolScriptWaitAsArray allow you to extract information from status messages issued by Jmol (including error messages); those aspects are explained in the level 3 guide, p. 114.

Including HTML code

It is often more convenient to pass HTML text without closing and reopening the <script> tags. To do that, you can use

```
<script type="text/javascript">
jmolHtml (" HTML text or content ")
</script>
```

Example:

```
<script type="text/javascript">
jmolHtml("this is <b>bold</b>.")
</script>
```

Or also to insert a line break using

```
<script type="text/javascript">
jmolBr()
</script>
```

which is a shorthand equivalent to `jmolHtml("<br>")`.

Coloring the model's panel

The panel for the molecular model (the Jmol applet) has by default a black background, well suited to contrast with all the atom colors and to provide depth perception. If you prefer another background color, you can set it before calling `jmolApplet()` with

```
<script type="text/javascript">
jmolSetAppletColor("color in hexadecimal format
#RRGGBB")
</script>
```

The format to set a color is the same used in HTML: the hexadecimal values of red, green and blue components (2 digits each), prefixed with the # symbol. It is also possible to use instead one of the color names predefined in Jmol (there is a listing in the appendix).

Example:

```
<script type="text/javascript">
jmolSetAppletColor("#FFC000")
</script>
```

applies a shade of orange (red: FF=100%, green: C0=75%, blue: 00=0)

We must insist: this command must precede that which inserts the model panel, jmolApplet(); further, if the page includes several panels, it will affect all the subsequent ones. As an alternative, you may change the background color for an applet after it has been inserted in the page, using commands of the scripting language (specifically, color background, p. 67).

Rectangular panels and panels with relative size

On the other hand, up to this point we have used square-shaped panels, but a model panel may have a rectangular shape using a small variation on the syntax for jmolApplet(). So,

```
<script type="text/javascript">
jmolApplet(300, "load acetate.mol")
</script>
```

inserts a square panel 300 pixels each side, while

```
<script type="text/javascript">
jmolApplet([300,500], "load acetate.mol")
</script>
```

inserts a rectangular panel, 300 pixels wide by 500 pixels high. (The syntax used is that of a JavaScript array with 2 data.)

Rectangular panels will generally make sense only if we want to display a molecule with a very elongated shape. If you choose to use them, you should take into account that, by default, Jmol will fit the model zoom to the longest dimension, therefore, depending on the orientation, part of the model may go off the viewable area. To get the model fit the shortest side, the scripting language has set zoomLarge off (p. 87). Future versions of Jmol might change the default option, so it is safer to always use explicitly `set zoomLarge off` or `set zoomLarge on` whenever you opt for rectangular panels.

The size of the panel may also be set in relative terms, as a percentage of the size of the window or the container element (a frame, a table cell, a `DIV` layer...). For that, it is enough to provide a value – or an array of two – as a percent or else as a number below one:

```
<script type="text/javascript">
jmolApplet("50%", "load acetate.mol")
</script>
```

```
<script type="text/javascript">
jmolApplet(0.5, "load acetate.mol")
</script>
```

in both cases, a panel is inserted covering half the width and height available. Or else

```
<script type="text/javascript">
jmolApplet(["90%","50%"], "load acetate.mol")
</script>
```

that will take 90% of the width and half the height of the container.

Including Jmol models in a web page - Level 3

Inserting radio buttons individually

In very particular instances, attaining the desired location of radio buttons within the page may not be feasible using jmolRadioGroup (which inserts them all consecutive). For these cases, another command may be used that inserts each radio button individually and assigns it to a group:

```
<script type="text/javascript">
jmolRadio("commands", "text displayed",
true or false flag, "separator after the option",
"name of the group")
</script>
```

Example:

```
<script type="text/javascript">
jmolRadio("spacefill on; wireframe off;", "spheres", false,
" ","a")
jmolRadio("spacefill 25%; wireframe 0.15;", "balls and
sticks ", false, " ", "a")
jmolRadio("color red", "bright red", false, "<br>", "b")
jmolRadio("spacefill off; wireframe 0.2;", "sticks", false,
" ","a")
jmolRadio("color cyan", "sky blue", false, " ", "b")
</script>
```

The result will be: ⊙spheres ⊙balls and sticks ⊙bright red ⊙sticks ⊙sky blue

where the three style options ("**a**") are linked in one part and the two color options ("**b**") in the other, and none of them is checked initially.

Handling the model based on JavaScript events (II)

In the level 2 section (p. 107) the use of `jmolScript()` was presented, as well as the simple use of `jmolScriptWait()`. This latter provides another utility: extraction of information from the status messages issued by Jmol, including error messages.

```
<script type="text/javascript">
var x = jmolScriptWait("commands")
</script>
```

```
<script type="text/javascript">
var x = jmolScriptWaitAsArray("commands")
</script>
```

When the function is assigned to a JavaScript variable ("x" in the example), this latter receives the status messages issued by Jmol while executing the *commands*, in the form of a single text string (`jmolScriptWait`) or as an array of text strings (`jmolScriptWaitAsArray`).

Analysis of that variable allows you to write JavaScript code that detects errors or other conditions and acts accordingly.

Inserting a "script console"

This tool provides the user of the web page with the possibility of passing commands to the Jmol model (which can be done in any case if the user knows the way to open the console integrated into the applet, unless the pop-up menu has been disabled by design).

The "console" in this case is made of a one-line textbox followed by a button; in the former, commands or scripts can be typed which will be executed on the applet when the button is pushed (clicked).

```
<script type="text/javascript">
jmolCommandInput("text displayed", size)
</script>
```

Where *text displayed* is the content of the button and *size* is the width (number of characters) of the textbox.

Example:

```
<script type="text/javascript">
jmolCommandInput("apply", 40)
</script>
```

The result is: [   ] apply

Saving and restoring model orientations

Several orientations of the molecular model may be stored into memory, assigning them an identifier:

```
<script type="text/javascript">
jmolSaveOrientation("identifier")
</script>
```

and restoring them at other time:

```
<script type="text/javascript">
jmolRestoreOrientation("identifier")
</script>
```

such restoration is instantaneous, but it may also be done using a gradual movement of the model, using

```
<script type="text/javascript">
jmolRestoreOrientationDelayed("identifier",
time)
</script>
```

time specifies duration in seconds of the movement that restores the model from its current orientation to that previously stored.

Browser test

The **Jmol.js** library includes a sophisticated routine for detecting the kind of browser being used to visit your page, in order to provide a warning if it is not compatible with the use of Jmol. The test is done automatically the first time a command is executed, but we may wish to check in advance and to provide a specific message or web page to be displayed when the test fails:

```
<script type="text/javascript">
jmolCheckBrowser("action", "URL or message",
"moment")
</script>
```

action must be one of these keywords:

- "popup" to open the URL address specified by *URL or message*, in a new browser window;
- "redirect" to open the URL address specified by *URL or message*, replacing the current page;
- "alert" to show a warning dialog (JavaScript alert) with the text specified by *URL or message*.

moment indicates when is the browser test to be done; it must be one of these keywords:

- "now" to test the browser immediately;
- "onClick" to test the browser the first time the user clicks on a control, for example a jmolButton();

default value is "onClick".

Pages with multiple models

Several Jmol panels can be placed in the same web page in order to simultaneously display multiple molecular models; you just need to repeat the jmolApplet() code at desired locations within the page.

In this case, it is important to specify which of the models each control should affect (button, menu, etc.). By default, controls act on the immediately previous model, in the order of page writing, but depending on the page design it may be necessary to state explicitly the link between controls and models.

Including multiple Jmol applets

By default, each call to `jmolApplet()` assigns a consecutive numerical identifier, starting at 0, which also, appended to the keyword "jmolApplet", forms the `id` and `name` parameters of the applet object in HTML. Instead, for easier management, you may assign a custom identifier when inserting the applet:

```
<script type="text/javascript">
jmolApplet( size ,  " commands ",  " identifier suffix ")
</script>
```

Example:

```
<table width="100%"><tr align="center">
<td>
  <script type="text/javascript">
   jmolApplet(250, "load a.mol", "left")
  </script>
</td>
<td>
  <script type="text/javascript">
   jmolApplet(250, "load b.mol", "mid")
  </script>
</td>
<td>
  <script type="text/javascript">
   jmolApplet(250, "load c.mol", "right")
  </script>
</td>
</tr></table>
```

inserts three Jmol applets, horizontally aligned using a table, in which three molecular models are loaded (files **a.mol**, **b.mol** and **c.mol**), and the applets are assigned identifiers "**left**", "**mid**" and "**right**". The respective HTML elements (<OBJECT> or <APPLET>, depending on the browser) receive "**jmolAppletleft**", "**jmolAppletmid**" and "**jmolAppletright**" as values of id and name.

(left)	(mid)	(right)
a.mol	**b.mol**	**c.mol**

Associating controls with applets

When you insert a control of type `jmolButton()`, `jmolLink()`, `jmolCheckbox()`, `jmolRadioGroup()`, `jmolMenu()` or `jmolRadio()`, the way to specify which applet its commands should be applied to is to use a previous `jmolSetTarget()` command:

```
<script type="text/javascript">
jmolSetTarget("suffix identifying the target")
</script>
```

Example:

```
<script type="text/javascript">
jmolSetTarget("mid")
jmolButton("spacefill on", "spheres model")
</script>
```

All commands after that – such as that of the button shown in the example – will be applied to the central applet, until a new `jmolSetTarget()` is set.

Associating commands with applets

Contrarily, `jmolScript()`, `jmolScriptWait()` and `jmolScriptWaitAsArray()` commands do not use the identifier set by `jmolSetTarget()`. Instead, they take an identifier suffix as their second parameter:

```
<script type="text/javascript">
jmolScript("commands",
"suffix identifying the target")
</script>
```

Example:

```
<script type="text/javascript">
jmolScript("spacefill on","mid")
</script>
```

The same procedure applies to those functions that save and restore an orientation (described in a subsection, p. 115, where this possibility was not presented to keep the explanation simple):

```
jmolSaveOrientation("identifier for the
orientation", "suffix identifying the target")
```

```
jmolRestoreOrientation("identifier for the
orientation", "suffix identifying the target")
```

There are yet a few utilities in the **Jmol.js** library, and extra details of those described in this handbook, which are not explained here because they are for more specialized use; for their description you are referred to the official documentation page, at http://www.jmol.org/jslibrary/

Integration with CSS (cascading style sheets)

The CSS style properties of the controls generated by **Jmol.js** may be unified using functions included in this very same library. (Alternatively, styles may be managed from the web page source code.)

The available functions are:

- **jmolSetAppletCssClass (***name of class***)** specifies the CSS class to be assigned to <APPLET> or <OBJECT> tags generated by jmolApplet() and jmolAppletInline().

- **jmolSetButtonCssClass (***name of class***)** specifies the CSS class to be assigned to <INPUT type="button"> tags generated by jmolButton().

- **jmolSetCheckboxCssClass (***name of class***)** specifies the CSS class to be assigned to <INPUT type="checkbox"> tags generated by jmolCheckbox().

- **jmolSetRadioCssClass (***name of class***)** specifies the CSS class to be assigned to <INPUT type="radio"> tags generated by jmolRadioGroup() and jmolRadio().

- **jmolSetLinkCssClass (***name of class***)** specifies the CSS class to be assigned to <A HREF> tags generated by jmolLink().

- **jmolSetMenuCssClass (***name of class***)** specifies the CSS class to be assigned to <SELECT> tags generated by jmolMenu().

All these functions take as an argument the name of a CSS class that is to be assigned to the element. The properties of such a class should be defined manually in the web page or in the associated style sheet.

Example:

`jmolSetButtonCssClass`("**bigButton**") assigns the class named *bigButton* to all the buttons generated by **Jmol.js**.

Appendices

Colors used by Jmol

Colors (CPK) for chemical elements

In Jmol, the default color pattern, or "CPK scheme" assigns a unique color to each chemical element. The back cover of this book shows them in color arranged in a periodic table.

The following table shows the atomic number, chemical symbol and hexadecimal color code (red, green, blue: RRGGBB).

1	H	FFFFFF	21	Sc	E6E6E6	46	Pd	006985
1	D,^{2}H	FFFFC0	22	Ti	BFC2C7	47	Ag	C0C0C0
1	T,^{3}H	FFFFA0	23	V	A6A6AB	48	Cd	FFD98F
2	He	D9FFFF	24	Cr	8A99C7	49	In	A67573
3	Li	CC80FF	25	Mn	9C7AC7	50	Sn	668080
4	Be	C2FF00	26	Fe	E06633	51	Sb	9E63B5
5	B	FFB5B5	27	Co	F090A0	52	Te	D47A00
6	C	909090	28	Ni	50D050	53	I	940094
6	^{13}C	505050	29	Cu	C88033	54	Xe	429EB0
6	^{14}C	404040	30	Zn	7D80B0	55	Cs	57178F
7	N	3050F8	31	Ga	C28F8F	56	Ba	00C900
7	^{15}N	105050	32	Ge	668F8F	57	La	70D4FF
8	O	FF0D0D	33	As	BD80E3	58	Ce	FFFFC7
9	F	90E050	34	Se	FFA100	59	Pr	D9FFC7
10	Ne	B3E3F5	35	Br	A62929	60	Nd	C7FFC7
11	Na	AB5CF2	36	Kr	5CB8D1	61	Pm	A3FFC7
12	Mg	8AFF00	37	Rb	702EB0	62	Sm	8FFFC7
13	Al	BFA6A6	38	Sr	00FF00	63	Eu	61FFC7
14	Si	F0C8A0	39	Y	94FFFF	64	Gd	45FFC7
15	P	FF8000	40	Zr	94E0E0	65	Tb	30FFC7
16	S	FFFF30	41	Nb	73C2C9	66	Dy	1FFFC7
17	Cl	1FF01F	42	Mo	54B5B5	67	Ho	00FF9C
18	Ar	80D1E3	43	Tc	3B9E9E	68	Er	00E675
19	K	8F40D4	44	Ru	248F8F	69	Tm	00D452
20	Ca	3DFF00	45	Rh	0A7D8C	70	Yb	00BF38

71	Lu	00AB24	84	Po	AB5C00	97	Bk	8A4FE3
72	Hf	4DC2FF	85	At	754F45	98	Cf	A136D4
73	Ta	4DA6FF	86	Rn	428296	99	Es	B31FD4
74	W	2194D6	87	Fr	420066	100	Fm	B31FBA
75	Re	267DAB	88	Ra	007D00	101	Md	B30DA6
76	Os	266696	89	Ac	70ABFA	102	No	BD0D87
77	Ir	175487	90	Th	00BAFF	103	Lr	C70066
78	Pt	D0D0E0	91	Pa	00A1FF	104	Rf	CC0059
79	Au	FFD123	92	U	008FFF	105	Db	D1004F
80	Hg	B8B8D0	93	Np	0080FF	106	Sg	D90045
81	Tl	A6544D	94	Pu	006BFF	107	Bh	E00038
82	Pb	575961	95	Am	545CF2	108	Hs	E6002E
83	Bi	9E4FB5	96	Cm	785CE3	109	Mt	EB0026

"Amino" coloring scheme for proteins

The back cover of this book shows this scheme in color.

The following table lists the standard abbreviation for each amino acid (the residue identifier in the **pdb** file) and its hexadecimal color code (red, green, blue: RRGGBB).

Ala	C8C8C8		Met	E6E600
Arg	145AFF		Phe	3232AA
Asn	00DCDC		Pro	DC9682
Asp	E60A0A		Ser	FA9600
Cys	E6E600		Thr	FA9600
Gln	00DCDC		Trp	B45AB4
Glu	E60A0A		Tyr	3232AA
Gly	EBEBEB		Val	0F820F
His	8282D2		Asx	FF69B4
Ile	0F820F		Glx	FF69B4
Leu	0F820F		other	BEA06E
Lys	145AFF			

"Shapely" coloring scheme for proteins and nucleic acids

The back cover of this book shows this scheme in color.

The following list includes the standard abbreviation of the amino acid (the residue identifier in the **pdb** file) or nucleotide, and its hexadecimal color code (red, green, blue: RRGGBB).

Ala	8CFF8C	Ser	FF7042
Arg	00007C	Thr	B84C00
Asn	FF7C70	Trp	4F4600
Asp	A00042	Tyr	8C704C
Cys	FFFF70	Val	FF8CFF
Gln	FF4C4C	Asx	FF00FF
Glu	660000	Glx	FF00FF
Gly	FFFFFF	other	FF00FF
His	7070FF		
Ile	004C00	A	A0A0FF
Leu	455E45	G	FF7070
Lys	4747B8	I	80FFFF
Met	B8A042	C	FF8C4B
Phe	534C52	T	A0FFA0
Pro	525252	U	FF8080

"Structure" coloring scheme for proteins and nucleic acids

This matches the interpretation of secondary structure type for proteins and the distinction between DNA and RNA. The back cover of this book shows this scheme in color.

Hexadecimal color codes are indicated (red, green, blue: RRGGBB):

α helix	FF0080	DNA	AE00FE
β strand	FFC800	RNA	FD0162
(β) turn	6080FF		
other	FFFFFF		

Coloring scheme by chain

In **pdb**, or equivalent, formatted files that contain more than one molecule in the chemical sense (for example, a double-stranded DNA or a protein with several subunits), the membership of each atom to one or another molecule is indicated by a chain identifier. Jmol may depict each chain in a different color; atoms in HETATM fields receive a darker tint.

Hexadecimal color codes are listed (red, green, blue: RRGGBB).

Identifier	color for ATOM	color for HETATM	Identifier	color for ATOM	color for HETATM
A, a	C0D0FF	90A0CF	O, o	00CED1	00B6A1
B, b	B0FFB0	80CF98	P, p	00FF7F	00CF6F
C, c	FFC0C8	CF90B0	Q, q	3CB371	349B61
D, d	FFFF80	CFCF70	R, r	00008B	0000BB
E, e	FFC0FF	CF90CF	S, s	BDB76B	A59F5B
F, f	B0F0F0	80C0C0	T, t	006400	009400
G, g	FFD070	CFA060	U, u	800000	B00000
H, h	F08080	C05070	V, v	808000	B0B000
I, h	F5DEB3	C5AE83	W, w	800080	B000B0
J, j	00BFFF	00A7CF	X, x	008080	00B0B0
K, k	CD5C5C	B54C4C	Y, y	B8860B	E8B613
L, l	66CDAA	56B592	Z, z	B22222	C23232
M, m	9ACD32	8AB52A	*none or*		
N, n	EE82EE	BE72BE	*numerical*	FFFFFF	FFFFFF

Recognized color names

These are a combination of RasMol and JavaScript colors. The listing indicates hexadecimal color code (red, green, blue: RRGGBB).

aliceBlue F0F8FF	darkSlateBlue 483D8B
antiqueWhite FAEBD7	darkSlateGray 2F4F4F
aqua 00FFFF	darkTurquoise 00CED1
aquamarine 7FFFD4	darkViolet 9400D3
azure F0FFFF	deepPink FF1493
beige F5F5DC	deepSkyBlue 00BFFF
bisque FFE4C4	dimGray 696969
black 000000	dodgerBlue 1E90FF
blanchedAlmond .... FFEBCD	fireBrick B22222
blue 0000FF	floralWhite FFFAF0
blueTint AFD7FF	forestGreen 228B22
blueViolet 8A2BE2	fuchsia FF00FF
brown A52A2A	gainsboro .... DCDCDC
burlyWood DEB887	ghostWhite F8F8FF
cadetBlue 5F9EA0	gold FFD700
chartreuse 7FFF00	goldenrod DAA520
chocolate D2691E	gray / grey 808080
coral FF7F50	green 008000
cornFlowerBlue 6495ED	greenBlue 2E8B57
cornSilk FFF8DC	greenTint 98FFB3
crimson DC143C	greenYellow ADFF2F
cyan 00FFFF	honeydew F0FFF0
darkBlue 00008B	hotPink FF69B4
darkCyan 008B8B	indianRed CD5C5C
darkGoldenrod B8860B	indigo 4B0082
darkGray A9A9A9	ivory FFFFF0
darkGreen 006400	khaki F0E68C
darkKhaki BDB76B	lavender E6E6FA
darkMagenta 8B008B	lavenderBlush FFF0F5
darkOliveGreen 556B2F	lawnGreen 7CFC00
darkOrange FF8C00	lemonChiffon ...... FFFACD
darkOrchid 9932CC	lightBlue ADD8E6
darkRed 8B0000	lightCoral F08080
darkSalmon E9967A	lightCyan E0FFFF
darkSeaGreen 8FBC8F	lightGoldenrodYellow FAFAD2

lightGreen	90EE90	paleVioletRed	DB7093
lightGrey	D3D3D3	papayaWhip	FFEFD5
lightPink	FFB6C1	peachPuff	FFDAB9
lightSalmon	FFA07A	peru	CD853F
lightSeaGreen	20B2AA	pink	FFC0CB
lightSkyBlue	87CEFA	pinkTint	FFABBB
lightSlateGray	778899	plum	DDA0DD
lightSteelBlue	B0C4DE	powderBlue	B0E0E6
lightYellow	FFFFE0	purple	800080
lime	00FF00	red	FF0000
limeGreen	32CD32	redOrange	FF4500
linen	FAF0E6	rosyBrown	BC8F8F
magenta	FF00FF	royalBlue	4169E1
maroon	800000	saddleBrown	8B4513
mediumAquamarine	66CDAA	salmon	FA8072
mediumBlue	0000CD	sandyBrown	F4A460
mediumOrchid	BA55D3	seaGreen	2E8B57
mediumPurple	9370DB	seashell	FFF5EE
mediumSeaGreen	3CB371	sienna	A0522D
mediumSlateBlue	7B68EE	silver	C0C0C0
mediumSpringGreen	00FA9A	skyBlue	87CEEB
mediumTurquoise	48D1CC	slateBlue	6A5ACD
mediumVioletRed	C71585	slateGray	708090
midnightBlue	191970	snow	FFFAFA
mintCream	F5FFFA	springGreen	00FF7F
mistyRose	FFE4E1	steelBlue	4682B4
moccasin	FFE4B5	tan	D2B48C
navajoWhite	FFDEAD	teal	008080
navy	000080	thistle	D8BFD8
oldLace	FDF5E6	tomato	FF6347
olive	808000	turquoise	40E0D0
oliveDrab	6B8E23	violet	EE82EE
orange	FFA500	wheat	F5DEB3
orangeRed	FF4500	white	FFFFFF
orchid	DA70D6	whiteSmoke	F5F5F5
paleGoldenrod	EEE8AA	yellow	FFFF00
paleGreen	98FB98	yellowGreen	9ACD32
paleTurquoise	AFEEEE	yellowTint	F6F675

Glossary

Sources cited:

- W3C: World Wide Web Consortium,
  http://www.w3.org/

- Wikipedia: http://www.wikipedia.org/

applet

- A program in Java, which can be executed by a browser. Also, any small program that connects into a system.
- In this handbook, **JmolApplet**, an implementation of Jmol that is executed only as part of a web page (in contrast, the **Jmol** application is the implementation used as a standalone program in the computer).

application

- A program prepared for a specific use, such as payroll payment, formation of a term database, etc.
- In this handbook, **Jmol** application, an implementation of Jmol that is executed as a standalone program in the computer (in contrast, the **JmolApplet** is the implementation used only as part of a web page).

Chime

- A program created by the MDL company (*Molecular Design Limited*, now integrated in *Elsevier*) to display molecular models interactively within web pages. Technically, Chime is a plug-in for the browser, and its operation is nearly identical to that of the standalone program RasMol, on which it is based. Due to its scant compatibility with several modern browsers, creation of web pages with Chime has been markedly reduced in recent years. Although Chime is available for free, it is a proprietary program, so it has not been possible to adapt it to the new browsers. Starting with version 10, Jmol was made compatible with the scripting language of RasMol and Chime so that it might become a substitute for the latter in web page development.

console

- A space where the user may type commands to be executed by a program. Jmol provides a console, similar in the application and the applet, accessible from the top and pop-up menus, where the program accepts all commands that form the scripting language and where information is displayed resulting from actions executed by the program.

CPK = Corey, Pauling, Koltun

- A color scheme used as a convention by chemists, based on colors of the popular plastic spacefilling models developed by Corey and Pauling, and later improved by Koltun.

CSS = Cascading Style Sheets

- "A simple mechanism for adding style (e.g. fonts, colors, spacing) to Web documents." [W3C]
- A style sheet language used to describe the presentation of a document written in a markup language (most commonly web pages written in HTML or XHTML). Used by both the authors and readers of web pages to define colors, fonts, layout, and other aspects of document presentation. It is designed primarily to enable the separation of document content from document presentation. [Excerpted from Wikipedia]

HTML = HyperText Markup Language

- The basic language underlying most web pages.
- The predominant markup language for web pages. It provides a means to describe the structure of text-based information in a document and to supplement that text with

interactive forms, embedded images, and other objects. [Excerpted from Wikipedia]

- "HTML is the *lingua franca* for publishing hypertext on the World Wide Web. It is a non-proprietary format based upon SGML, and can be created and processed by a wide range of tools, from simple plain text editors to sophisticated WYSIWYG authoring tools. HTML uses tags such as <h1> and </h1> to structure text into headings, paragraphs, lists, hypertext links etc." [W3C]

Java

(Java is a registered trademark of Sun Microsystems, Inc.)

- A language to build programs that may be used independently of the operating system employed by the user's computer.
- A programming language originally developed by Sun Microsystems and a core component of Sun's Java platform. Java applications are typically compiled to bytecode which can run on any Java virtual machine (JVM) regardless of computer architecture. [Excerpted from Wikipedia]

JavaScript

(JavaScript is a registered trademark of Sun Microsystems, Inc. It was used under license for technology invented and implemented by Netscape Communications and current entities such as the Mozilla Foundation.)

- A programming language that allows one to write web pages whose content is modified interactively depending on the user's actions.
- A scripting language best known for its use in websites (as client-side JavaScript), but which is also used to enable scripting access to objects embedded in other applications. Despite the name, JavaScript is essentially unrelated to the Java programming language. [Excerpted from Wikipedia]

mol

- Molecular coordinate file format used in the software by the MDL company (*see* Chime). It is also called "MDL molfile". It is frequently used in other environments, for small size molecules. Includes coordinates and bonds, limited to 1000 atoms. Allows several models in a single file (a variant named **sd** or **sdf** format).

PDB = Protein Databank

- The major international database storing structures of proteins, nucleic acids, complexes between both and some other macromolecules. It is freely available at no cost through internet, at http://www.pdb.org/

pdb

- Molecular coordinate file format used by the PDB; it has become one of the standards even outside that database. Recent versions of the database advocate its substitution by **mmcif** format, with better capabilities, but the use of the latter is still much less widespread. It includes a great amount of information on each atom, residue and molecule, in addition to the coordinates. One of its variants allows several models within a single file (used, for example, in NMR experiments).

RasMol

- A program to display molecular models interactively on personal computers, with a functionality similar to Jmol[1]. It is only implemented as an application, or standalone program, (the equivalent "applet" incarnation would be the Chime plug-in). It is available for free (http://www.rasmol.org/) and recent versions are open source under GNU-GPL license.

  Note 1: Version 11 of Jmol incorporates numerous capabilities absent in RasMol, particularly in specific areas such as crystallography, vibration, orbitals, surfaces, drawings and management of variables.

xyz

- A file format frequently used for small-size molecules. It was originally designed for the XMol program from Minnesota Supercomputer Institute, but it has been copied or adapted to many other environments. It includes only coordinates, but some extensions have been developed that include, for example, vibrational information. It allows multiple models in a single file.

Reference web addresses

http://www.jmol.org/
   Jmol web site. It is the main point to access all information.

http://wiki.jmol.org/
   Jmol Wiki (a space for exchange among the community of users).

http://chemapps.stolaf.edu/jmol/docs/
   "Interactive Scripting Documentation", a complete reference guide for Jmol command or scripting language (linked from the web site).

http://wiki.jmol.org:81/index.php/Literature
   Publications describing Jmol or its use (part of the wiki).

http://wiki.jmol.org:81/index.php/Websites_Using_Jmol
   Compilation of web sites that use Jmol (part of the wiki).

http://wiki.jmol.org:81/index.php/Journals_Using_Jmol
   Compilation of journals that use Jmol to illustrate their articles (part of the wiki).

http://wiki.jmol.org:81/index.php/Books_Using_Jmol_In_Figures
   Compilation of books that use Jmol to illustrate their content (part of the wiki).

http://biomodel.uah.es/
   The author's web site: *Biomodel – páginas de complemento al estudio de bioquímica y biología molecular* (Biomodel: pages for complementing the study of biochemistry and molecular biology). Includes a few sections in English.

http://biomodel.uah.es/Jmol/
   Section devoted to several aspects, rather technical, of developing materials using Jmol. Includes material in English.

http://biomodel.uah.es/Jmol/manual/
   Companion web page for this book; it will include some accessory materials, correction of misprints, updates, etc.

Index of commands and keywords

www.ingramcontent.com/pod-product-compliance
Lightning Source LLC
LaVergne TN
LVHW042336060326
832902LV00006B/214